My Psychic Eyes

Katie Coutts

Peter Grose Ltd

Published by
Peter Grose Ltd
Monmouth

Printed and bound in Great Britain by The Bath Press

ISBN: 1-898-88525-7

Contents

To Mum — *For everything*
To Alan — *For loving me*
To Miss Nats — *For her love and support*
To Bill — *For being my friend*
To Gail — *For her help*
To Gilly — *For her patience*
To David R. — *For having faith in me*
To Peter and Ros — *For the future*
Last but by no means least, to my readers: — *Thank you*

Chapter I
The Early Years

I was born in 1965 under the fiery sign of Leo. My family was a close one—mum, dad, two older brothers and myself. I guess my family were very ordinary. No seventh daughter of the seventh daughter for me. I was the only girl, and the youngest of three.

Dad was a hard working man, a painter and decorator to trade. Mum was a bookkeeper. As siblings, we were and still are very different. My oldest brother is very ambitious and very successful. My other brother is a comedian, and not ambitious. Neither of them have any psychic ability—or not that they are aware of.

My psychic ability comes firstly from my mum, but more so from her mum, my darling gran, who died in 1982.

Gran never really took her ability seriously. The most she did, and she did it regularly, was read tea leaves. Almost always what she said was correct, though she was never very impressed with herself for saying it.

Her other daughter, my mum's sister, is psychic too, but doesn't take it seriously.

We are very Irish in that both my parents' parents are Irish. I have always had a great affinity for the people of Ireland

and for the land itself. I believe my psychic ability stems from this Celtic background.

I don't think I'm overly privileged. To my mind, everyone has some gift and some strength. We have people born to sing, people born to dance, people born to be maths teachers and people, like myself, born to use the paranormal—or to introduce the paranormal to others.

I am told constantly that the first sign I showed of having this ability was when I was around age six. Apparently I said Prince Charles will never be king. I don't remember this personally.

I didn't really become aware of my ability until the late age of 14 or 15. And I was pretty much the last to know. Everyone else who knew me realised there was something different about me. They remember me telling them things about themselves that even they didn't know—though they later found out that I had been right.

I never intended or, if I'm honest, never thought about using my ability in a professional manner. Truthfully, I didn't like using it at all. I know now that this was due to a lack of confidence, not so much in my ability but in the way I could use it. Despite this shyness, people quickly began to notice. They put a catalogue of my predictions together until they had a huge portfolio. When so many of them proved correct, I was the only one who wasn't impressed.

I don't remember much about these times. I wasn't frightened. I just didn't think I was particularly different, and I couldn't see what all the fuss was about.

I left school at sixteen, a total rebel against any sort of authority, wanting to marry and have children. I was not academic. Or, to quote my teachers: "She has it, she simply refuses to use it."

I vividly remember my parents telling me I'd regret my wanton ways. They said that my school days were the best of my life. I did not and still do not agree with them, nor do I regret any of the decisions I took. I hated school. Studious? Not me, or certainly not in any academic way.

It wasn't until the age of 24 that I thought seriously about whether I should put my psychic ability to use. Could it be that I could do some good with it, by helping others? I hoped so.

I had moved to Fife by this time, was married and had my darling daughter Natalie. I had many jobs—I suppose you could describe me as ambitious, or at least money oriented. If such a business as shopping ever existed, I'd be managing director. I loved spending money—often money I didn't have.

Some of the jobs I liked, some I hated, and some I learned to enjoy. Most were doing some fantastic enterprise on my own. As much as I hated having teachers, so I hated having a boss. I'm one of those people who hates routines and hates having anyone tell me what to do.

My pub work was the best. I loved it because it fitted in with my family and allowed me to have a social life as well as a salary. I wooed my customers, and never failed to earn more money in tips than in wages. Looking back, those were some of my best times.

Office work never appealed to me. I did six months as a telephonist and hated it. I did work as a car hire receptionist and left after four days.

No, I wanted a job where I could work the hours I wanted

and do the work I wanted to do. I just didn't know what that work was. So I battled on, coming up against dissatisfaction after dissatisfaction. I always had hope. I knew one day I would find the perfect job.

Next I attempted a domestic cleaning business, and had a few years of great success. I employed staff, and then employed some more. This was an amazing time. I was earning good money, was my own boss, had employees to order around, and won a business woman award. Trouble was, it just didn't feel right. I did not belong. Something was missing.

In 1990 my mum suggested I "do readings" on a professional basis. I didn't think this was a good idea, and put it aside.

Then a close family friend bought me a pack of Tarot cards. At the time I humoured him, and told him I'd take a look at them.

When I did get around to studying them, I couldn't believe how fascinating they were. I don't think people realise how profound and very, very apt Tarot can be. It is an ancient way of giving the right advice. Tarot cards truly are an incredible find.

(Having said all of that, I don't use Tarot much now in my readings. I use them only as a focal point and because the querent feels comfort from them. I'm often surprised, however, to note just how accurate they are—accurate in that they often coincide with my own psychic vibes, which I rely on wholly.)

Another year or so passed and I finally relented. I agreed to carry out some readings at a friend's house. I was so nervous.

I felt like a fraud. However, the readings went very well and everyone commented on how accurate they were.

I did the same thing a couple more times, and then decided to place a small advert in a local newspaper. I still had my business to run, so I didn't have a great deal of time to spare.

The response to the advertisement floored me. Soon I was booked up for three, four and then six months ahead. I didn't notice at first how fast this new business was developing, and how much more confident I felt in my new career. It just snow-balled while I wasn't looking!

It was then that I knew I had to do something about it. I couldn't keep my other business going and find time to meet the demands of my psychic clientele. So I sold my cleaning business and decided to use my psychic ability on a full-time professional basis. From that day to this, I have never looked back. I don't regret what I did. In fact the only regret I have is that I didn't do it sooner.

My family were very supportive—they thought I had wasted too much time and should have turned professional a long time ago.

My husband was great, for he had long since abandoned his sceptical attitude. He'd been forced to face up to the facts. How coincidental was it that I'd relay events from his day, *before* he had a chance to tell me about them? How coincidental was it that if he had any pain, say toothache, I'd have it too and tell him how much he was suffering! Furthermore, I had given him a reading not long after I met him and I think he is still reeling from it.

Alan is less complicated than me. Having been raised in the country, most things to him are black and white. Well, until he met me! Black and white I am not. I'm one of life's analysers. I like to know the ins and outs of absolutely everything.

Nonetheless, he very quickly came over to my side. Proof was all he wanted and boy, I gave him all the proof he could handle. He is now a total believer, in me and in the paranormal in general.

All my family were delighted with my progress. But I'd say my in-laws took longer to get used to the idea of having a "psychic" in their midst. Some of them are still a bit nervous, I think, but that no longer upsets me. Long ago I stopped feeling I had to impress people. If someone doesn't believe in my ability, then that is their prerogative. Personally I think it is fear rather than rational doubt which drives most sceptics to reject the paranormal.

How did I feel about my new career? Well, to be honest, it just happened, and for a long time I didn't have any real feelings about it at all. I've said that I'm a born analyser, but the one thing I never try to analyse is my work.

I don't believe anyone should attempt to find out how the paranormal functions. If they did, and found the answers, the very word paranormal would have to disappear. My dictionary defines it as "beyond normal explanation", and that's how it should stay. I don't believe that we are supposed to poke and prod to find the answers to the mysteries of the paranormal. If someone found all the answers, we would no longer have such a fascinating subject.

I find the intrigue and awesome interest in the psychic world by so many millions of people totally enthralling and exciting. I don't want anyone to break that spell—at least not in my time!

So I say: leave it alone. Use it, but don't try to explain it.

Although there is a widespread fear of the paranormal, I don't think people are afraid of me. They're more intrigued. However I do know some are terrified of thinking too deeply when I'm around, in case I "tune" into them.

Surprisingly enough, I find that men I deal with are more afraid than women. Women are very strong, and can take anything you say to them. Men don't like to hear bad news.

However I think my most successful readings are with men, and for a surprising reason. Men are so open. They don't know how to put up a front when their life is sprawled out in front of my eyes. Women, on the other hand, have a great ability to cover things up.

I'm asked often if I have to be secretive about my work, in case people might be afraid of me. The answer is no. I tend to be very open about my work, although I do hate the sometimes awkward silences when a person I've just met doesn't know what to say.

I can see the cogs turning in their mind, and I wonder if they are tongue-tied because they are afraid. Or do they want to know something, and can't think how to ask the right question? Or, worse, are they sceptical? Being a Leo, I can't take criticism very well, nor can I take anyone's sarcasm.

I absolutely hate having to explain myself, or give a blow-by-blow account of my work. I've only recently developed an attitude, arrogant as it may sound, of not wanting to be forced to "prove" myself. I watch others in my profession on television, being ripped up and getting lost for words as they try to tell the sceptical interviewer what he or she wants to hear. I don't feel a need for that. I now want to concentrate only on those who want what I have to offer. Those who don't can continue their lives without me.

The sceptics of this world don't want to believe, so I for one have stopped trying to convince them. It matters not how many bits of proof I have given them. They still have their smart fixed ideas and don't want to hear the evidence.

I'm delighted to do a reading for someone who has faith, not only in the paranormal but in me personally. These are the people who deserve a glimpse of this wonderful world. As far as I'm concerned, the sceptics can hang as they grow.

And no, I don't believe I am burying my head in the sand. I just don't want to waste any more precious time on having to prove myself or having to explain everything. Every minute I spend trying to convince others could be better spent relaying experiences and messages to people who want to hear.

I want to spend my time productively on what I believe I have been sent to do—to use the paranormal, firstly in an interesting way, and secondly in a way that benefits my clients.

Chapter II
Turning Professional

I first worked at age 12, when I very illegally did an Avon round. This was to enable to me to visit my relatives in Canada, who had come over that year. It was the first sign of ambition. I planned to save 15 pence a week, innocently thinking I would quickly save the money needed to go to Canada. I've not yet made that trip, although it is still the one country I feel I want to visit.

My first real job was in a lawyer's office in Glasgow. I was sixteen, fresh from school and hopeful of my future. I worked as a telephonist and it was here that I realised my career had to involve people. I have never been a behind the scenes type of person. I much prefer being out there in front, dealing with and talking to the public.

While I was working in that office, I had some very strange dreams. For many, many nights, I dreamt I had given birth to a beautiful daughter. The dream was so real that I could physically feel this wee bundle. Six months later, to my horror, I realised I was pregnant. My career as a telephonist ended abruptly, as I left for life as a mother.

My beautiful daughter Natalie was born two weeks after my 17th birthday. She is now fourteen years old and the single most precious thing in my life. Like me, she is very psychic.

I get quite amazed when she voices my thoughts or when she does something I was thinking about doing. Like my mum, Natalie has a lot of dreams, and they usually have some bearing on the future. They almost always come true.

I don't think Natalie will follow in my footsteps as a professional psychic. Her plan at the moment is for a career in journalism. Somehow I think she will stick to that choice.

When I was ready to return to work after Natalie's birth, I found a job in a pub. I adored it, although I had no inclination then or now to own my own pub. I love people, and by looking at them I can usually tell what kind of person they are—what their tastes, dreams and attitudes might be. I had many psychic vibes whilst working in the pub.

Everyone who knew me in those days also knew that I had this ability. At that point I had no idea where it would lead. Often I'd be asked to do quick readings on colleagues or customers, and I usually obliged. I can't say I enjoyed giving readings then, for I wasn't comfortable with the idea. Confidence came only after I decided to turn professional and had the benefit of experience and constant use of my powers.

Nonetheless, I did do some readings and I remember quite a bit of what I told them and of their subsequent comments.

One man who was heavily into body building asked me if he should give up his job and tackle body building as full time career—perhaps coaching eventually. For whatever reason—and at that time I didn't know why—I found myself having very bad vibes and advised him under no circumstance to consider this. Not only that, but his body building days would be brought to a rather sinister end within a matter of months.

I was told some months later that this poor guy had been in

a car crash and had severely damaged his back. Through time he was able to return to his full time job (which thankfully he hadn't given up) but the body building had to be stopped as it could have caused irreversible damage.

I met him some years later and he was fit and healthy looking. He told me he was still able to exercise a great deal, but lifting weights was out of the question.

Another prediction involved a pregnancy. A girl, whom I remember being very fond of, asked me to do a reading. She would have been around the same age as I was—in those days 20 or 21. Her very short marriage was on the rocks and she asked if she would divorce her husband and find someone else. Her husband was much older than she, and wasn't the nicest of people.

I predicted a few things for her which seemed to make sense, but my next prediction was puzzling. I saw her very happily remarried to another man. At the time of the reading she had no children, so I was confused when I saw her marrying this man complete with child—a child which was not her new husband's. This confused her too, for she had no plans for children. However, a few months later, weeks after she had finally decided to leave her husband, she discovered she was pregnant—by her husband.

Thankfully she stuck to her resolve and did not go back to her husband. Three months after the baby was born, she met and fell in love with her new husband (not new now, for they have just celebrated their eighth wedding anniversary). They have two other children and are blissfully happy. We both agree those days seem like another world as both our lives have changed so much.

I suppose word did spread about my ability, but still I had no

11

plans to do anything differently. Using my gift as a career did not enter my mind. I continued to carry out readings for friends and colleagues but nothing else.

For the next few years, working in pubs and clubs was my social life and my career. The one thing that kept me going was Natalie and the thought that one day I was bound to find a way out of this rut.

It wasn't until 1984 or 1985 that I really started to notice that my powers were unusual.

My darling dad died in March 1985, and this hit the family dreadfully. We reeled from shock, stuck together, and moved on with our lives.

The following year, minus Natalie, who was being well looked after by my mum, I decided to make my first trip overseas with a girlfriend. It was intended to be a holiday for laughs and a carry on.

It was a holiday which changed my life.

On our very first day, sitting sunning ourselves by the pool, in walked this gorgeous guy. This was Alan, and I instantly fell in love with him. We hit it off right from the start, and although his holiday was nearing its end and mine only beginning, we parted at the airport full of promises to write to each other when I returned home. He lived in Fife, St Andrews, and I lived in Barrhead, Glasgow. It turned out that distance was no object, for we met up the week after I came home from my holiday. We visited one another every weekend for eighteen months. Then we married, and I made my move to Fife.

I still believe I would never have changed my career if I had remained in Barrhead. So I have a lot to for which to thank both Alan and Fife.

My brother followed me through to Fife, and met and married a local girl. Then, some years later, my mum came too. The one sadness I have is that we now have very few ties left in Barrhead.

Alan has always been very supportive of my psychic ability and I think is jolly relieved that I have finally found something which has enabled me to settle down.

During the early years of our marriage, I did almost every type of job involving people ever invented—from working in a local pub, to door to door selling, from car hire to other kinds of selling. Once again, looking back, I see the familiar pattern of all my jobs heavily involving people.

Those days were frustrating for me. No matter which job I did, and no matter how much I enjoyed it (and I'd say I enjoyed each and every one of them), I still felt I didn't belong. I knew I had a calling. I just didn't know where or what.

It wasn't that I was no good at the jobs—they just weren't good for me. I was told often that one day I'd find not only what I was good at but, more importantly, I would find something which would feel right. Looking back now, I realise my forte was staring me in the face. I just couldn't see it.

After I was given the Tarot Cards as a Christmas present in 1990, I slowly began to listen to my family, who for years had been telling me to consider using my psychic ability professionally. I thought: "What the heck, I've tried everything else". So, I spread the word around my friends and family, and within months realised I had never been so happy in my work. I had never felt so much that at last I belonged.

I can't honestly say it was a slow start, because within months my diary was full. I travelled a good bit in those days, all round Fife, Edinburgh, Glasgow and up North. Then the press began to take notice and I was having articles written about my skills. Next, the famous began ringing. I loved the attention. I loved my work, and the buzz it gave me.

I didn't pretend, and still don't pretend, to know what it is I have, for I don't understand it fully. One very reputable psychic told me in my early days that if I tried too hard to find the answers, I could risk losing my powers. So from then until now I just do my work, and I question none of it.

At the time I was amazed by the support I had from family and friends, who had become really fed up with my changing jobs. Every time I changed, I would say: "This time it will work. I've found my forte at last." Eventually everyone switched off, and although they wished me well, they were now reserving their judgement about each new move.

So it came as a great surprise, and I took it as an omen, that they were so encouraging and eager to see me succeed in this new line of work. I, too, have never had any regrets about the change. I've loved every minute of my job and am hugely excited about my future.

One of my most asked questions is: what do I see, what do I feel, what do I hear, when I have a psychic vibe? Well, every psychic is different, but for me it is firstly a mere feeling. I sense things. I feel actual emotions, and even physical pain.

One of the very few readings I have been unable to do—and I think there have only been three such incidents in my whole career—had me feeling so bereaved and saddened that I simply couldn't give my client a reading.

It happened around 1992. I had gone to a client's home, and I was getting on really well with the guests who had come for readings. My vibes were flowing and, by all accounts, everything I was saying to each person was spot on.

Then a young girl of around 21 came in for her reading. I felt a huge sweep of sadness which almost brought tears to my eyes. My heart was heavy, and I felt as though I was in mourning. Hard as I tried to concentrate and tune into this young girl, I just couldn't. I felt an overwhelming urge to cry.

These feelings, although unusual, were not foreign to me and I knew something dreadful had happened to her in very recent times, possibly only days or weeks ago. I told her what I was feeling and how I couldn't tune in to her.

I felt slightly panicky, for I didn't really know what I was saying. I only knew I couldn't go on. Through tears and heartache, the poor girl told me her father had died in her arms only a week ago. This explained why I was feeling that way. She was distraught, and therefore so was I.

A similar incident occurred a few years later when a lovely but very sad looking lady came into my office. As soon as she sat down, I was engulfed with imaginary flames and I began to cough as smoke went into my lungs.

I did manage to carry out this lady's reading, but it was so difficult. I felt anger and rage coming from her, and a profound feeling of guilt. I knew she had nothing to feel guilty for, but still the feeling came.

Her story was very tragic, for her daughter had been trapped in a house fire and despite my client trying to save her, the child died. This explained everything, from the smoke and flames to the guilt. The poor woman was punishing herself and blaming herself for her daughter's death.

Truth was, the fire had started during the night and was solely down to an electrical fault. It had absolutely nothing to do with the mother and there was no way she could have prevented the tragedy.

One of my regular clients always seems to give me physical pain when she comes for her readings. I can't explain why, but according to her it has happened on all four visits she has made to me.

I seldom remember any of my readings because, as my psychic vibes come, I seem to go into a different mode. I can literally feel myself taking a deep breath and before I have exhaled, another voice inside me begins the reading. It's quite a weird sensation.

The first time I did a reading for this girl, I felt a burning pain at the base of my neck. I told her about it and she admitted she too had this pain often. In fact, she was suffering the pain at the time. It left her for the hour she was with me—while it transferred to me! Then after she left it began on her again, and left me.

The next reading, around 18 months later, saw me develop such a bad headache that I had to interrupt my reading to take pain killers. At the time, she told me, she had been suffering a three-day migraine.

The next time, and we laughed before the reading as we recalled the last two readings, I had a great pain down near one of my ovaries. Naturally she too had this pain, and had given it to me.

Sadly this wasn't something to laugh about, as she was currently pregnant. The pregnancy failed because she was carrying the foetus in her fallopian tube. During that same reading, however, I was able to predict another child and a safe pregnancy within fourteen months. Thankfully that happened as per my prediction.

I remember one of my earliest readings had me a little afraid. As I was waiting on my client coming, and I remember it

vividly as a cloudy Monday morning, I had an awful sensation, as if someone was strangling me. The feeling was not
pleasant, for it was literally as if someone had their hands, or
some rope, tightly around my neck.

I couldn't understand it then, although I now know if I am
feeling such "inexplicable" experiences that it has to have
something to do with an imminent reading. I was quite right,
for not long into the reading, I had the spirit of a very disturbed lady, who turned out to be my client's mother, who
had committed suicide by hanging.

Some feelings are not quite so sinister. Some are quite funny.
I had one recently where an old man, and yes, I could actually
see him, was sitting in an old battered-looking arm chair. It
was apparently his favourite chair while he was alive. In fact,
the family used to joke to him about burying him in the chair—
hence the significance of it in my mind.

The feeling I had this time made me giggle, for it was as if
someone was tickling me. I told my client this, and she looked
amazed. The old man used to sit in the armchair and, when
his grandchildren visited him, he couldn't get up and play
with them. So instead he would invite them onto his lap and
tickle them. This held great significance to my client. As I
proceeded with the reading, every now and again, I'd feel
him tickling me.

Another very funny incident involved a spirit who was, by
all accounts, quite stern while he was alive. I had accused
him of this to my client, his daughter, and I felt him literally
kick my shin in protest at my description. Then I could hear
what sounded like a stick being hit against stone. My client
told me that he would sit banging his cane against the fire
surround, which was made from ceramic tiles.

Although I'd admit to hearing more often than seeing through my vibes, I have often had imagines, like a moving picture in my head of events. It's rather like looking through a lens, perhaps on a camcorder. I find myself turning my head as if to see something slightly hidden.

I have grown to realise that if a picture or scenario in my head is fuzzy, then I'm being told the event is further away in time, whereas if the picture is absolutely clear, then I know the event in much closer—maybe even a matter of weeks away.

Interestingly, if and when I see my spirits, as opposed to merely hearing them, I tend to see only their back. I seldom see faces, although if there is anything of great significance, like a birth mark, then I'll see that. Or, if they wore something unusual like horn rimmed glasses, I'd get to see that.

So, as to what actually happens, I'd have to say primarily I sense, then I hear, a voice—usually a strange voice. I've always been under the impression it is the voice of spirits belonging to my clients—perhaps one of their family who has passed away. I also see events which, as I've explained, very often appear like a whole load of scenes which move and blend. It's a bit like a moving picture—sometimes jerky and sometimes smooth and fluent.

When it comes to seeing and hearing spirits, or people who have passed away to the other side, again I'd say I hear them far more often than I see them. For some unknown reason, they seem always on my right and, if I hear them, they are behind my right shoulder. If I do see them, they are to the front of my right side.

Their faces are never clear. They are always blurry but, as I've said, I don't always get to see them front on—they tend to have their back to me, especially if I'm seeing the whole of them and not just their face.

I think you'll find all psychics and clairvoyants make this same point: it is profoundly difficult to describe what we see, feel and hear. It doesn't seem at all strange to me, but trying to relay it in a plausible way is almost impossible.

The spirits manifest in a normal way, in that they simply appear. They exit in the same way, too. The vision of their face simply disappears. I haven't seen any walk through walls or closed doors.

Some experiences I've had, where I believe it is my own family "visiting" me, can only be described as perfectly normal. Although I don't always see the door opening, I can hear a door opening. I don't believe ghosts walk through walls. Mine certainly don't.

Chapter III
Personal Experiences

I'm often asked what sort of experiences I have myself. Many! Wonderful and often "weird" things happen all the time.

I often have vibes and premonitions from something as simple as watching television. Most, although not all, are on a personal level, or concern my life in some way.

I watched a news bulletin some years ago involving the firm my father worked for, and had a premonition that it would soon shut down. Sadly, within six months of my prediction the closure was announced, and my home town reeled with grief. I also predicted that the entire factory would be demolished, and this took place more recently. The Yorkshire Imperial Metal Company no longer exists ... the factory is now a piece of waste ground.

Many different things spark off a psychic reaction, and I find myself helplessly tuning in to pictures and hearing voices of premonitions. I always write everything down, both by way of proof and to allow me a clearer picture on what it is I'm visualising.

I can only describe my psychic state as if another is within me. I can clearly hear my own voice, but to me it sounds like someone else. Because of this, I hardly ever remember what I've said or how it came about. I'm fully alert when this happens, but I just don't seem to be "me". I'm not afraid. To me, it's just part of my life.

I have a great respect for the dead and would never impersonate or ape them. They seem to respect me, too, and respect my privacy. I often see spirits moving around in my office, which is an extended part of my house. The office is separated from my lounge by a huge glass door, and I see movement and hear laughter beyond the door. But these spirits never come in to the lounge. As I don't recognise any of them, I can only assume they belong to clients I've seen earlier in the office.

I would admit to being slightly afraid at some of these events, but only when I've come down from my psychic state and am "normal" again. I have never felt afraid of spirits during my readings with clients. Another psychic explained that my fear may well be down to my youth.

My own loved ones from the other side visit me often. I can hear them and, on the odd occasion, I have the pleasure seeing them.

My husband was slightly afraid initially when I saw his father. At this point, I hadn't seen so much as a photograph of my father-in-law, but that would not have mattered for I was seeing him as a much younger man.

I was able to describe his looks, manners, and even his sense of humour. I saw an old car dated around 1969, and was able to describe a knee problem he had. After some thought, my husband was really rather pleased to discover his father was watching over him. He felt immense comfort from this.

My own father has come over to me mainly via other medi-

ums, as I have had very little chance of seeing him personally. I can't quite fathom the reason for this. I wish I could.
On the odd occasion he has appeared, he always has the same
expression on his face, and he also seems to be constantly
rushing. He never stands still, and looks terribly busy.

Two other family members have also seen him, and again he
appears to be rushed. When he appears at our family home,
he never leaves the hallway. It would seem he is unable to
venture any further. Again, this one bamboozles me.

Lots of my premonitions come during sleep. Some come in
the form of dreams which then manifest into reality. Others,
more commonly, come as I'm nodding off. In the interval
between full consciousness and a sleep, I have flashes and
feelings about future events.

Once, I could hear and smell fire. I could see a street not too
far from where I live, and could clearly see flames and smoke
belching from a huge tank. I was still awake, for I rose from
my bed and walked to my window, where I have a view of the
street and this tank. All seemed normal and, although it was
dark, I'm sure I would have noticed fire. Two days later I read
in the local newspaper that the road had been closed due to
the tank overheating, and the fear of it exploding.

This incident reminds me of a night, many years before, when
I was around 11 years old. I lived in a different area then, and
found I couldn't sleep on this particular night. Once again, I
was seeing fire. At this young age I wasn't aware of how my
psychic ability worked, and I was slightly afraid. I could hear
banging and could smell smoke. Upon investigation from the
window, I saw no sign of fire in the night sky.

The following morning I told my family about my experience, but no one else had heard anything. Later that same day

we were told of a fire in a factory some four miles away. It had been a bad fire, and the factory was completely destroyed. It wouldn't have been possible to hear and smell the fire at such a distance. It could only be explained by my psychic powers.

Smaller, more insignificant premonitions occur. Lots, I suppose, could be put down to intuition, but not all. I often have flashes of future changes. For example, a local shop which had once been owned by a glazier suddenly in my mind looked more like a bakery. Not long after, the shop was sold and a baker took over. (He is there to this day.)

When I first moved to my present home, I remember parking my car and walking to the mall. As I did this, I had visions of the car park as a tunnel, or perhaps a railway line. I could see a high wall and two wide strips of road or rail. Within three years, the car park area was demolished and in it's place, a bypass was built. This new road has a tunnel as part of it's development.

The offices of the *Daily Record,* prominent on the banks of the river Clyde in Glasgow, also came into my list of premonitions. One time, travelling home and crossing the Kingston Bridge, I remember saying to my husband that this impressive building would not be there much longer. One year on, plans for the premises to be moved further down the motorway were announced.

I'm often amazed by the clear vibes I get when I'm meant to be "switched off". One such incident happened when I met friends for lunch and we were joined by another couple I hadn't met before. I immediately felt vibes coming from the man, Alan, and wasn't quite sure what to say and what to leave out.

Both Alan and his wife insisted that I tell them what I was

feeling. I felt quite mortified, but as they were insisting I had no option. I tried to be tentative, but the ferocity of my words was unmistakable.

I felt Alan had to leave the area, for I could see no further happiness for him. I was surprised to see that his wife had a completely different outlook, and didn't feature in her husband's future. I also felt that he was panicking over some situation about which I could only feel doom.

I could clearly see infidelity, which doesn't make for a great conversation during lunch, especially with a stranger. I therefore felt uneasy about mentioning this.

It further became clear that this was the reason Alan must leave. I initially assumed he would leave through a lack of opportunity, perhaps in his present career, but as my vibes unrolled a completely different picture emerged.

Not only had he been unfaithful, he had also impregnated his mistress. I just didn't know how to bring this out. How on earth could I tackle such a tender and embarrassing topic?

However, the crowd were insistent, and I had to say what I was feeling. Alan blushed a lot, but his wife took on a calm, almost resigned look. I quickly tried to change the subject. This time the crowd had no objection.

I was later told that what I had said was fact. Alan had an affair, and the girl was indeed pregnant. His wife was suing for divorce and the mistress was chasing him, along with her four brothers. Alan had no option but to leave the area, firstly for his own safety, but also to protect his wife from any more pain.

On a cheerier note, I was approached one time at a local dance by friends I hadn't seen for some time. Linda, one of my old friends, asked constantly about my work and asked outright if I could see her having a child. Apparently she had been trying for four years.

I tried to tune into her over the din of the band and was amazed when I found this relatively easy. I had never met her husband and was able to describe him to perfection. Linda's mouth hung open just at that. I was able to tell her of the pain she was feeling at not being a mother, and also of the two miscarriages she had suffered. I was also able to tell her, because I clearly saw, that she would have a son and he would be born in 16 months' time.

The evening passed and, as often happens, the subject is changed and folk generally make light of what I'm saying. Don't get me wrong, most people are hugely fascinated by my line of work and I've found very few scoff. But we had many more subjects to cover, so we all had a dance, a good time and parted as the night came to an end.

I never gave the discussion further thought and didn't see Linda for two years. I met her whilst shopping, and with her she had the most beautiful wee bundle of blue in her arms.

My prediction had been correct. She had fallen pregnant seven months after we had met at the dance and had given birth to her baby boy nine months later, making my prediction of childbirth 16 months later quite accurate.

Chapter IV
Kindred Spirits

Many people, and not just professional mediums, have had experiences with spirits. It's a subject that everyone finds interesting—even the most ardent sceptic.

I'm often asked how I know spirits are around me. There are many ways of knowing this. The most common has to be sensing. I can just simply tell if I'm not alone!

I see them too, although this is far less frequent. I can often smell some aroma which is of significance to the spirit. For example, I once had a spirit accompanied by an overwhelming pong of Swarfega, the stuff garage mechanics use to clean their hands. My spirit, who was my client's deceased husband, had been a mechanic to trade. She instantly knew why I said I could smell Swarfega.

Another time, I had the spirit of a lovely and kind lady, the mother of my client, and this time I could smell what I could only describe as the sweeties, Parma Violets. This made sense to my client as her mother always wore the same perfume, similar in smell to Parma violets.

I can never touch my spirits, although I often feel them touch me. I had an example only two nights before I write this. Often I find myself working during the night, when the house is quiet and the family are in bed. (I've become a bit of an insomniac since I began my career as a psychic.) Several times I've had the feeling of urgency, as if a whole gathering of spirits don't want me in the office—which is an extended part of the house. I can't be sure whether they want me to go to bed to avoid exhaustion and "burning out", or if they are saying: "This is our patch now, get out!" The former probably.

I don't feel afraid, but I do find myself hurrying to move out and allow them the space they seem to need. This only ever happens very late at night or, should I say, in the early hours of the morning.

I can't say I ever feel afraid, because I don't. It may be that I've been doing letters or readings only minutes before and I've had a giggle with a spirit—so fear doesn't come into it. But at these particular times what I do feel can be quite overwhelming.

I find it very difficult to describe what I actually see and feel. If I do see a spirit, it's as if I am looking through a lens or having a moving picture in front of me. The spirit can manifest in many different ways, from the classic white blur to a mosaic type outline, to just a face, to a person as real as you or me.

Another question I'm often asked is: can I hear them and can anyone else hear them? I certainly hear them, either through what I would call my adviser or the actual spirits themselves—or I assume it's them anyway. I say "them" because I can often differentiate between accents. No one else hears them.

I'm often surprised at mediums who can all work together in groups—I can't do that, for I'd get vibes from everyone and be thoroughly confused. I marvel at the way they can hear one voice each—I'd be totally bamboozled!

I can point out that I see a spirit—say, when I'm out socially. I'll tell the company I'm with to watch for a certain thing happening. That way they, too, know there is a spirit present. Let me give you an example. We were staying at a hotel with friends and as we all sat in the lounge of the hotel, I clearly saw a small, Jewish-looking man walk into another room. I told my friends this and further told them that the man would walk back out of the room. When he did so, they would see the coal fire, which was raging, flicker.

This is exactly what happened. As they all sat transfixed, glaring intently at the fire, they too saw the flickering and the logs on the fire collapse into ash. It was an amazing scene— almost like a wind had blown on the fire. This, of course, was merely the spirit walking past the fire.

I don't know that I altogether believe spirits can walk through walls. I feel that may be a myth. It's my belief that spirits are not as complicated as all that—they are surprisingly normal. If they could walk through walls, then why do so many people experience things like doors being opened by spirits? If they could walk through walls then there would be no need to open doors! I feel they may simply be able to manifest—in other words they just appear and that's that. Some make a grand entrance, and some do not.

I was recently told an amazing story. A local lady had been in hospital and was so ill the medics feared she might die. However, she rallied round and although she hasn't yet made a full recovery, she's well on her way to doing so.

The total amount of time she spent in hospital was eight

weeks and during that time she became friendly with the nurses and other patients. She remembers one nurse in particular as being extremely nice. This nurse apparently looked after her so well and way beyond the call of duty that she thought often about her—even after she was allowed home.

This lady decided to send flowers and chocolates to the nurse—so moved she was with the care and attention given. However, when the parcel arrived, addressed to the nurse in question, it was revealed that the nurse died some nine years ago. Imagine the shock and surprise this patient felt at being nursed by a ghost.

Another tale which I loved concerned a friend of mine. Her father had died only months earlier, when she was convinced she saw him in a High St chain store. As my friend walked toward the exit of the store, there, in all his glory, stood her father, watching her. She instantly walked toward him but found he turned his back and walked away. He walked right out the big glass doors and by the time my friend got outside, he was nowhere to be seen.

My friend, although convinced of what she saw, at first put this down to her mind playing some kind of trick. Then she met Michael.

Michael was an old family friend who had emigrated years before. He had known the family well. One of the first questions Michael asked was how her father was. She was about to tell him of her father's sad departing when he began to tell her how he had spoken to him in the High Street—by this time, a week before. Putting two and two together, my friend realised this was the same day she thought she saw her father.

Michael, having been away from the town, hadn't heard of her father's death.

One letter I received from a very distressed reader, Jane, told of much the same story. This time it concerned her mum, who had died after a long illness. Although everyone was deeply saddened by her death, at the same time there was general relief. The poor woman had suffered quite dreadfully.

Jane had gone into the chemist only ten days after her mum had died and was told her mum had to finish some details on her prescription. Apparently her mum had been in to pick up her prescription four days previously and hadn't completed the prescription details. Two chemist assistants shuffled embarrassedly—both aware of Jane's mum's death. The chemist himself, however, a locum, didn't know the family nor of the mother's death. As Jane tried to explain, the chemist was embarrassed but remained convinced of the woman's visit.

He showed Jane the prescription and indeed it did have her mum's signature on it. To all intents and purposes, Jane's mum had walked into the chemist, picked up the prescription, filled out some of the details on the reverse of the paper and walked out again. The chemist remembered her vividly, for they had briefly talked of the weather and of Jane's mum's garden (a subject she spoke of constantly when she was alive). He was able to tell Jane roughly what the woman wore, and it all sounded like the deceased woman. There has never been an explanation for this, but somehow Jane's mum got her prescription and had a brief conversation six days after she died!

Fiona had been so proud of her mum. Her dad had been dead less than a year and her mum decided it was time to move on. They had been a close couple—married for over 40 years. Fiona's mum began her new life taking driving lessons, and although struggled with all this new learning, she was determined to succeed. She'd speak of buying herself one of those wee "bubble" cars. She thought they were cute and had decided she would feel safest driving one. Then she died!

The family reeled from the shock at losing both parents within such a short time of each other. It was the general opinion that, although the mother had put on a brave front, she in fact missed her husband of so many years that she died of a broken heart.

Roughly six weeks after the death of her mother, Fiona was driving to work but was stopped at a junction as an elderly lady tried to manoeuvre her car—almost into Fiona's path. Fiona first saw the car, a wee "bubble car", and this immediately brought memories of her mum flooding back to her. Then she saw the driver—it was her mother! The car was the very same colour her mum had planned on buying.

The lady driver smiled at Fiona and then simply drove off. Fiona turned her car around and started speeding in the direction her mum had gone. As she rounded the corner, she was sure she would see her mum, for that particular part of the road was long and straight and you could see the road ahead for about half a mile. However there was no car. This was odd because her mum or any other driver could not have driven fast enough to be out of view in such a short time.

All of this just shows that spirits are not only seen as white shadows. They can be very real indeed.

Chapter V
Problems: Mine and Others

The paranormal seems to be much more openly discussed nowadays, with articles in newspapers and magazines, and television programmes, looking seriously at paranormal phenomena. Everyone, even a sceptic, is fascinated by it. Those who treat it cynically are, in my opinion, merely afraid.

More and more evidence is building up to prove there really is a lot to the paranormal. Life after death, out of body experiences, predicting the future and other unexplained phenomena, all seem to be on the increase.

I'm still fairly confused about why I am psychic and why I was chosen to do the work I do. But I firmly believe we each have a "gift" of some kind which we should use in our daily life as a career. We see people like Shirley Bassey who are born to sing. Sharron Davies was born to swim, Billy Connelly to make us laugh. It seems I was born to guide people, and to answer some of the very many questions which arise from the incredible world of the paranormal.

I can't always explain why, but I do try to explain what it is I am seeing, feeling, hearing and so on. I defy scientists or sceptics to explain what I'm doing. The dictionary defines the paranormal as "beyond ordinary explanation", and I worry that if scientists do come up with explanations and answers, the paranormal will become extinct.

So it is with great joy that I thank all those who persuaded me to use my psychic power in this way. I am so glad my friend bought me my first pack of Tarot cards.

I have had years of joy and happiness from my work as a Psychic Consultant. I have discovered many different aspects of the paranormal, and the more I channel and use my psychic energies, the more I have returned to me.

Although my work as a Psychic Consultant has almost always brought happiness, it can also bring problems for me as well as for my clients. For instance, one of my spirit visitors just about convinced my family and friends I was having a nervous breakdown ...

Two sisters came to see me for a prearranged reading. They had lost their mum only months before, and the first time they came I remember feeling overwhelming grief. Without even trying to tune into them, I asked them if they could make another appointment four months later. Something told me I shouldn't read for them at that particular time. They were both surprisingly relieved by this—bearing in mind they had already waited eight months to see me.

Four months passed and they duly returned. I had seen many clients in between, but as soon as they walked in, the feelings I'd had on the previous visit came flooding back. I couldn't ask them to leave again—this wouldn't have been fair. So, against my better judgement, I decided to give it a try.

I knew as soon as I began that I was going to have difficulties with them. They were perfectly nice people, but they were simply torn apart with grief over the death of their beloved mother.

I carried on with the reading, which took me almost two hours instead of the normal 30 minutes. My head was pounding and I felt most unwell.

Half way through the reading, the mother came to me from spirit. Nothing unusual in this, it happens regularly throughout my readings. She duly passed on her messages in exactly the same way as all my other hundreds, if not thousands, of spirits.

It was only when I finished reading for the first lady that I knew I could not carry out a second reading for her sister. She understood, and seemed relieved. She told me that although she thought she had been very prepared for the reading, when it came to the crunch she was too frightened.

I thought nothing more about this, although I do remember feeling hugely tired—a sweeping exhaustion had enveloped my entire body and mind.

It seems I suffered some kind of blackout and, although I functioned normally, my family and friends who came into contact with me certainly noticed something was wrong. I didn't appear unwell, but I certainly did appear tired.

More frighteningly, my mind wandered. I spoke to people on the phone and sounded slightly slurred. One friend in particular thought I was under the influence of drink! My cousin phoned and I asked how her baby was—the baby which was not due for another three months. Apparently I'd say one thing one minute and then repeat it word for word the next.

My husband was quite frightened for me. By the second day he realised this was something more than just normal forgetfulness or tiredness. He thought I was having some kind of mental breakdown.

I remember very little of those two days—an exceptionally strange feeling in itself. All I then remember is this:

A friend had come over to do some work for me in my office, and I left the house saying I was going to another friend's house with a message. I did indeed reach the other friend's house, but as I walked in I apparently said I didn't know why I'd come. I then turned about and drove the half a mile or so home. Dangerous now, I realise.

When I arrived back home, my friend asked where I had gone. I could not remember.

The next thing I recall was waking up and rising from the armchair (this was approximately 30 minutes after I had gone to sleep). I saw my friend working in my office, which is an extended part of my home divided by a glass partition. My husband said I seemed to be angry and asked why she was there. Did they think I was incapable of doing my own job? It seemed as if I was resentful, and as if they were giving me charity.

Then I went up to bed and I could clearly hear everything going on downstairs. I suddenly felt very frightened, and I remember thinking: I have Alzheimer's disease.

Shortly afterwards I saw four figures in my room. Bear in mind I was fully awake, for I could hear my family talking downstairs. The four figures were known to me—my father was one, my gran another, her brother, and the fourth, a baby— I instinctively knew it was the child I had lost two years previously.

Dad walked over to where I was lying—stealthily, as if trying to calm me. He bent down, kissed my forehead (I can still feel his touch) and as he stood up, he was gently leading an old lady from me—as if she had been inside my head. He said only this, "All will be well now Kathleen. You are safe again."

It was clear from that moment that my dad and other close family members had come to clear whatever it was that had happened to me. My husband found me ten minutes later with silent tears streaming down my face.

I did some research into this and my findings explained a lot. What happened to me was quite amazing.

The mother of my two clients had died after a few years of suffering from Alzheimer's disease. She, too, had been very resentful of the family's help—she had been such an independent woman. At times her mind cleared, so she disbelieved the truth of her illness. She often cried, because she could not understand what was wrong and why everyone wanted to do things for her. This would explain my anger at my friend's help.

I also spoke to my doctor about it, who cleverly explained that the spirit of my two clients' mother must somehow have lodged in my body. I then temporarily suffered her ailments. This could well be true, for I regularly suffer symptoms of my clients. If one has a bad back, toothache, or whatever, the pain is transported to me until the reading ends.

I'd never had a spirit lodge into my body before, and the doctor explained that the reason is simple. I was apparently so tired and stressed at that particular time that I simply wasn't sharp enough to keep the spirit at arm's length the way I had done, albeit subconsciously, every other time.

He described the body as being like a car. If you don't put in water, oil, and so on, the car is bound to seize up. It wouldn't be likely to blow up, for there would be warnings, such as smoke. The brain is very similar to that. I hadn't been giving it enough attention and therefore it was throwing a message at me.

No one can know what would have happened to my brain if I hadn't had this warning. It would be wrong to surmise a stroke would occur—but whatever would have happened, I'm only glad I had those signs.

I can usually spot a sceptic straight off, for they carry what can only be described as a wall around their aura. Very visible to the psychic, I might add. I often can't quite decide what to do about these people for, if I'm in a confident mood, I reckon I can change their minds by proving my psychic ability to them. On the other hand, if I'm not feeling so confident, then I may look as if I'm slightly mad!

Undoubtedly, and understandably, I have to realise I am on "show" most of the time. There is no room for error. Human nature expects me to be correct one hundred percent of the time. So people jump on the occasional incorrect prediction, no matter how many correct predictions I make the rest of the time. I admit to feeling exactly the same way about other psychics. It's still very much a case of seeing is believing.

The following encounter with a sceptic began as just another social evening with six of us, three couples. To me, however, for the entire night, there was a seventh guest. At first I was unsure who the lady was. I knew I was the only one aware of her presence. She was as clear to me as the other people and, although she spoke to me very little, I knew she was listening to every word being spoken.

She told me her name was Sarah and that she was the grandmother of David, one of the guests. She told me she died 11 years before, and her death was the result of a stroke.

Within an hour, the inevitable happened. I was asked questions about my work. I let everyone speak and ask their questions as I watched David smiling and looking cynical. He appeared bored with the subject, and I could see he didn't believe a word of the conversation.

I'm renowned for my "way" with sceptics. I like to keep them hanging and then I pounce. This method has served me well over the years and, without sounding too conceited, I generally convince the sceptical client.

David was such a case, for once everyone else had heard enough, I turned to David and told him his gran was standing next to him. He continued to look unimpressed and, no matter how much information I gave him, he remained steadfast in his scepticism.

I was beginning to run out of things to relay, and I couldn't hear anything else from the old woman.

I hate being beaten, and I admit to getting quite stroppy when a sceptic appears to be winning. So I urged the old lady to say more. It was like a childish game.

Thankfully she did say more. As I passed the new information on, David began to believe me. He admitted later that he had been fairly sure of me from the beginning, because some facts I came out with surprised him. I, of course, had been too intent on relaying my "evidence" to notice his transformation from sceptic to believer.

I do so hate to be disbelieved and can't help my need to prove myself. I realise it's not necessary. But as with all artists, I like to be perfect at my job.

Pauline, a girl with whom I had recently become friendly, sat having a chat in my lounge. We discussed all the usual things women do. I could tell she had a huge secret, and one which affected her psychologically. I was sure she didn't realise just how badly. She said nothing to me about any of this. Instead she spoke about various issues in her life, mostly general things rather than anything too personal.

I listened, but couldn't stop these persistent vibes. I felt pain and distress coming from Pauline, and began to have flashes of her as a child. As you can imagine, it was difficult to take in what she was saying, for so many other things were going on in my mind. She continued to talk on and on. In fact, she was evidently very highly strung and hated awkward silence.

The morning passed, and I have to admit to feeling relief when she left. Later that day the flashes I had experienced in the morning came back. This time Pauline was slightly older and seemed to be pushing someone away from her. There was no mistaking the fact that the girl in my mind was Pauline, though much younger than the girl I had been chatting to earlier that day.

The younger Pauline seemed very distressed and shouted viciously at the man she appeared to be fending off. He was a huge man, and very much had control over Pauline. She was hysterical, and yet he seemed so calm. I found this scene quite disturbing, for it was as if I was reliving the entire scenario. It became clear to me that the man was attempting to rape Pauline. She was lashing out, kicking and screaming, but he took no notice.

The scene in my imagination instantly changed, and I then saw Pauline crouched in a corner. Although she was the same age as in my first scene, she was now behaving like a young child. She was sucking her thumb and her body was swaying rhythmically. Her face was sodden with tears, and her dress badly ripped. I shall never forget the sheer sense of grief I felt while I watched Pauline in this state.

Days passed before I saw Pauline again, and I wasn't sure whether I should mention my experience to her. I decided I should, and tentatively broached the subject. She listened carefully, and I couldn't fail to notice how her expression took on a twisted, contorted stare. This in itself was not only disturbing but also confirmed that something dreadful had happened during her childhood.

It was fairly obvious to me what this something was, and she didn't need to explain. Pauline had been sexually assaulted by her father from the age of four. The picture I was having in my mind turned out to be the last day this terrible, recurring event had taken place. I described to Pauline all that I had seen, and she remembered it well, down to the dress she was wearing. It was the one which I saw had been ripped during the assault.

She was 14 years old and had told an aunt all about the horrific assaults her father had been making for almost ten years. She knew by this time that what he was doing was wrong and she said she felt, for the first time, compelled to tell someone. She knew only that she wanted this time to be the last. The aunt could not have doubted Pauline's word, for she saw the distressed state her niece was in. She also saw the torn clothing.

Thankfully Pauline's aunt took immediate action and the man was sentenced to some years in prison. He has since died, but Pauline has been left scarred by the ordeal.

I'm not sure how Pauline felt about my seeing all of this. I do know, however, that she has since seen a therapist and has lost the gaunt, disturbed look on her face. Any time I see her now, she seems happier and appears be enjoying life. She isn't as highly strung as she was when I first met her, so the therapy must have helped her.

I have been approached by her aunt, who commented on how I had helped Pauline, for she was in what psychiatrists call denial. Now she has been forced to confront her past, and the results can only be beneficial.

A similar incident occurred with Jean. People often don't realise just how complex the mind and all it's functions are. In Jean's case, her subconscious mind had allowed her conscious mind to think it had forgotten or shut out an entire chapter of her childhood. Because these incidents were disturbing, it suited Jean to think these memories were gone and that the incidents never took place. She simply did not allow herself to think of them.

This is not, of course, how the mind works. The unconscious and subconscious mind store up memories and then release them into the conscious mind. These memories often catch us off guard, and can be the main reason people become depressed and unbalanced.

Jean's story is a rather sad one. She and her brother, who was only one year older, had become involved with a group of kids who stole and vandalised. Jean and her brother went along with the crimes rather than risk becoming victims themselves. From the age of 11 Jean stole from shops, handbags and anywhere she could. Her brother did the same.

They continued to pursue these crimes for two years, until events got out of hand. Whilst on a shoplifting spree, Jean and her brother were caught and taken to a police station. You can imagine their fear. As a result of this, Jean immediately stopped stealing and moved on to a different set of friends.

Her brother was not so lucky, however. He continued to keep the thieves as friends, and before long the crimes became more sinister. Jean quickly noticed the difference and identified their now more frequent stealing as a way to feed and pay for their drug habit. Jean's brother denied he had a problem and still refused to stop seeing his friends.

He rapidly changed into a Jekyll and Hyde, and lost what little direction he had in life. His school work suffered and Jean was powerless to help. He was arrested many, many times but nevertheless continued his life of crime. Jean's entire family felt helpless, but no one could stop him.

Jean's brother died from a drugs overdose, and the family reeled with grief, both for their son and brother and also with regret for the way his life had turned out. The only way Jean could cope with this grief was to protect herself from any further hurt, and the only way she knew how was to become a recluse.

By the time Jean came to me for a reading she was 35 years old and had led the life of hermit. Both her parents had died, and she had no close family or friends left. Friends and colleagues had tried to include her, but gave up when she didn't seem interested. Jean's life consisted purely of work and her lonely home.

During the course of Jean's reading with me, all of her past heartache came out. I was overwhelmed by many aspects of it. All of her deceased family, her brother, her parents came over from spirit and all had their various messages.

Jean's brother had most to say. He spoke in great detail about

43

the remorse and sorrow he felt over everything he had made the family endure. Jean seemed delighted by the messages I was passing on, and told me she had never felt anger, only pity, for her brother.

One thing the trio of spirits felt strongly about was the lonely life Jean was living. They told me how artistic she was, and how she really should use her talents. They also wanted her to have a husband, and a normal life.

Jean looked sad as I mentioned this, and I could see she wished her life could be different. She had become so stagnant and afraid of other people that she could see no way out.

I felt strongly that Jean could have a far better life, and advised counselling. I told her that I could not counsel her personally, but could recommend someone who could perhaps hypnotise her and take her back to the beginning. He could show her a very different path to follow, and possibly change her life.

At first she seemed uninterested. I was deliberately insistent and even cruel to her. I was fully aware of what I was doing, and I wouldn't have continued if I felt it would prove futile. I felt, on the contrary, that my words might well change Jean's entire life. None of her spirits disagreed with me.

Eventually I could see Jean absorb my words. She was with me for almost four hours, so you can imagine how absolutely exhausted we both were by the end. I felt drained, and was unable to function for the rest of that day. I had a huge sense of peace and harmony, however, so I knew my efforts would be well rewarded. And how they were.

Jean had taken in what I said and sought the help I thought she needed. She received various sessions of hypnotherapy, and they paid off. She didn't contact me for a long time after the initial consultation, preferring to receive her treatment alone. I thought a lot about her but never interfered or tried to contact her. I knew she would come back to me when she was ready.

The therapy helped enormously, and was the main turning point in Jean's life. Jean managed to start living a normal life. She told me how difficult it was, and I'm not surprised. After all, she had never changed or felt emotion since the young age of 14. She had, in effect, missed out on her youth.

It has taken Jean a full four years to get her life together again, and she has relived all the grief and pain caused by the deaths in her family. She never allowed herself to mourn while living her secluded life. Now, she has managed to mourn and feels this helped her to come to terms with all that had happened.

The best news is that Jean is soon to marry a lovely man, and I just know they'll be blissfully happy. Tom, Jean's future husband, knows everything that has happened in her past, and has been a huge comfort.

This all just proves how we should not brush problems under the carpet because, without fail, they will re-emerge and cause untold damage.

These last two stories show how readings, whether they are spiritual or futuristic, can bring real benefit to people's lives.

Death has affected all of us in some way. For some people it is devastating, and they never recover. I've had hundreds of letters from widows, orphans, mothers who have lost their child— all finding it difficult to come to terms with death.

Death is never easy, for although we are all supposed to believe that life is but a training ground for the "real thing"—

Heaven, and that we are all only on loan, I doubt any of us get any real comfort from that.

We spend our lives sharing and loving those closest to us. So how can we be expected to be philosophical when they die? Who in their right mind will be able to say, "Okay, they've gone now, I won't miss them, I won't mourn them and I won't cry for them"? Utter nonsense. Of course we cry for our loved ones. Try telling a widow who's been married to her childhood sweetheart for 50 years, that she shouldn't cry—after all, he was only on loan to you!

Therefore, when I can give any comfort or solace to my client, even just a little, it makes my job so very worthwhile. I never tire of this, no matter how small the sign may be. My grieving client may want only to know their loved one has arrived in Heaven. They may want to know if their gran has her eyesight back, or if their toddler has found another child to play with. The whole thing is profound and desperately sad.

It is so wonderful to be able to pass on some message of hope. And this hope can literally make the difference between life and death for my client. Lives are shattered by death. Whole families are torn apart. The griever does not know where their loved one has gone, what they are feeling, thinking, or what they are doing.

I have never felt able to ask any of my spirits where they are or what it is like. As I've said before, I can hear and listen to my spirits, I can even see them from time to time, but it seems I can't talk to them. I can't ask them questions, but instead just have to listen to what they have to tell me.

Chapter VI
Casebook: Working With The Future

M ost of my predictions begin with the use of psychometry—psychic vibes whereby I hear, sense and often see my way through my readings. Each and every reading is therefore completely individual.

So how do I go about my work?

I find I mainly sense and feel vibes coming from my client and then, literally as if by magic, my predictions come flowing out. I still find the whole thing quite amazing. I often feel pain as well as emotion coming from my clients.

Before I can start, I have to make psychic contact with the person. It's here that I find the crystal useful. I ask my client to hold a crystal and, once it is returned to me, I then seem able to tune into their thoughts and feelings. Next I see flashes of incidents which lie ahead for them. Obviously I sometimes see similar incidents for others but, in the main, the reading relates to my client alone.

The best way I can describe how my powers work, is to say firstly that I seem to have an "on/off" button. To switch on, it is imperative I am relaxed.

The switching off process is more difficult. As with any mentally draining job, trying to return to a relaxed state is very difficult. This can often cause problems, for if I'm out socially and obviously relaxed, then my "button" seems to think it's time to switch on. I can be sitting having dinner and, unbeknown to the diner at the next table, I have vibes coming from him, either reading his mind or having flashes about future events concerning him. I can just imagine his face if I ever walked over and told him what I was thinking!

I also find that if I'm in company and friends are talking about my work, I seem to switch on and be in a position to predict some things for them. I have to admit that I have never had so many invitations in my life as I now have!

I do find it much more beneficial if I'm able to come up with some fascinating facts that are so personal to the person that they have no option but to believe in what I'm saying. This usually has the desired effect—all attention is on me! Born under the Sun sign of Leo, my need for the limelight is immense.

I have found that the paranormal now reaches all types of people. Whereas once only those seeking guidance would believe in what I do, now the most stable, affluent and contented man is likely to come for a reading. I have read for many different people, from different careers and different cultures. Everyone is interested and mostly everyone believes, or in my experience, is at least prepared to listen.

Psychic readings can sometimes take unexpected turns. I began one reading by telling a friend of an ear operation. She did not remember this and, I think, disbelieved me. When my friend asked her parents about this, they confirmed it to be true. Apparently her grandmother died the very day my friend was admitted to hospital for the operation, perhaps explaining why she had forgotten.

I also predicted two other major events for this same friend. I warned her of romance abroad. Normally a very strong person, my friend would be completely in awe of this chap, I said. I felt he would mistreat he and may even steal from her. He would most definitely, at the very least, lie to her.

The following year she visited Greece and, as per my prediction, met and immediately fell for this man. They saw a lot of one another, and she arranged the remainder of her holiday around him. Then she began to notice that she was paying all the time. He made one excuse after the other about why he had no money with him. He'd tell her he couldn't get his travellers' cheques cashed, or he had run out of his hotel in a bid to meet her on time—just one excuse after another. She cannot understand why she believed all his lies, but he did exploit her temporarily naive nature.

On the last night of the holiday, she left him for an errand and, when she returned, her bag and all its contents were gone. As this was her last night, she had cashed in all of her remaining cheques and had a substantial sum of money in her purse. He had stolen the lot. She never saw him again.

The good news was my other prediction. I foretold of another relationship which she would find within six months of the holiday. This time she would find "Mr Right" and they would marry and be very happy. They are now married and are, as I said, very much in love.

Penny came to me very unsure of where her career was going. She was a very bright young lady. At twenty five she had already surpassed her own expectations and those of her counterparts. She felt she needed a change of direction and another firm had offered her some fabulous prospects. I immediately felt very negative vibes about this new firm and advised her to wait a further six months before making her decision. She felt very disappointed, and I'm sure she initially disagreed with my advice. In fact, without telling me, she left the consultation determined to go ahead in her own way. She proceeded with her plans, and went as far as signing some contracts.

In the throes of this, she came back for a further consultation. Again I felt the same negative vibes. I couldn't help what I felt and I tried to assure her that I had to tell the truth. I couldn't give her good news if I didn't see good things ahead. I had to tell her how I saw it in reading.

I felt Penny would be let down at the last minute and, although everything was signed and sealed, she would not able to change the outcome. She would not move to that particular firm. However she would have an even better offer within two weeks and, long term, the benefits would be far greater. Again, as with the first offer, this second, better opportunity would come to her. She would be offered a post which she should accept.

As she left, she still felt the first offer would be the one she would accept. She could picture herself working for the firm with which she was currently negotiating, though I felt she would go for the second offer.

Within a further three weeks, she came back. Now she really did have a dilemma! The first offer was about to fall through. The firm in question was undergoing a takeover and all recent transactions were in jeopardy.

I still maintained that a second offer was about to come her way and that she should forget about this present one. She did not want to hear this as her hopes were pinned on the first.

What happened? Penny was let down with the first offer but, within two weeks, another offer came her way in the manner I had predicted. She is now very content in her new post and there is talk that the other firm may well be closing down altogether.

One of the joys of my work is having clients come back to me to share their good news. I made a very special prediction for Alison Ogilvy from Surrey that she would soon give birth to a bouncy, healthy baby boy. This was particularly good news for her, for she and her husband had been childless for 14 years. She had received medical assistance such as IVF, but nothing had worked.

As with so many of my readings, I immediately felt overwhelmed by excitement. I often feel real emotions when doing a reading. Alison was quite rightly slightly cynical of my prediction. She had long since passed the stage of grasping at straws. She had her hopes raised and then dashed so often that she took what I said with a pinch of salt.

However, as predicted, Alison gave birth to her beautiful son only eleven months later. She and her husband were so overjoyed that they asked me to be godmother. They truly felt I had put some kind of "good luck" vibe on their infertility.

Of course I could not take any sort of credit for this, for it was purely coincidental that Alison's consultation with me should fall only weeks from her pregnancy.

She asked me if I would have still seen this happy event if she had come 14 years earlier. My answer would be a definite "yes". I may also have been able to save them a lot of time and money by telling them that their first child would take so long, but that it would come, and it would happen naturally.

Stuart, the baby, is now about to celebrate his first birthday and he is one beautiful little boy whom I hope will have a happy and healthy life. (I haven't predicted anything to suggest otherwise, so all should be well.)

I remember my feeling of happiness when I attended the wedding of a young couple for whom I had previously done a reading. Jane, the 20 years old bride-to-be, had been diagnosed as having cancer of the throat. She had just finished her chemotherapy treatment when she first came to see me.

I could quite clearly see the traumatic few months she had endured, but was delighted to tell her that I could see no more cancer in the future. This, it transpired, had been the medical opinion too.

Jane was, as you can imagine, still very afraid and although she was glad to hear everyone try to reassure her, she remained sceptical.

Then, three months before her big day was due to take place, she was asked to go into hospital for more tests. Apparently some discrepancy in recent blood tests had worried the doctor.

Everyone held their breath in fear as we all waited for the results.

Jane was immediately admitted to hospital, where she remained for four days while they carried out gruelling test after gruelling test.

The poor girl was terrified. Instead of preparing for her wedding day and experiencing all the joy and delight entitled to her, she was instead lying alone in hospital bed feeling frightened. I reminded her of the reading I had given her, and tried to reassure her that this was some mistake. I continued to feel positive vibes, and could only pray that my initial prediction was correct.

The great news was that Jane was given the all clear. The doctor explained that the complication was due to nothing more than a viral infection.

The wedding day was delightful, the bride radiant. The sun shone as if declaring all would be well for the young couple. No more ill health has befallen Jane, and I believe it never shall.

Nellie and Evelyn came to me while at a crossroads in their life. Neither knew what lay ahead and, although both were extremely outgoing and talented, they had no idea how to utilise this in their life. They simply lacked opportunity, so their lives had pretty much stood still.

Nellie was a red headed nut, (she won't mind my saying that about her, she was just so funny and adventurous) while Evelyn was creative and intelligent.

For two close friends, they really had very little in common. However, a better combination you could never meet. They had such an affinity, and I could feel the electricity flow between them. The difference between their natures left me feeling confused, yet at the same time intrigued.

Nellie had the gift of the gab and was undoubtedly the conversationalist of the two, while Evelyn was the business brain.

Their natures and talents apart, I predicted an intensive training course and a huge amount of success.

Time-wise I forecast 100% profits in the first two years. I could see a small site for their beginning, but within the first two years I could clearly see much larger premises. Both girls were creative, one with design and the other with craft. I could see colours, wood, craft, knitwear, porcelain and many other fabrics and material.

The potential seemed endless and the market keen. Their enthusiasm was enormous. Never mind my predictions, these girls couldn't fail. All they needed from me was to find their starting point.

That was 1991. Now in 1994, the girls have a super reputation land a business which employs 20 staff. They supply goods to many overseas countries and their future couldn't look better. They have outlets all over Britain and are now well on their way to earning their first million. Thank goodness they came to me for a reading.

David was a nice client whom I saw for a reading twice. He was in a bit of a state the first time he came to me. His wife had left him and had taken his beloved son with her. So I was glad to see his reading was offering him quite a bit of promise. Within two years he would be well on his way to rising out of the mess he was currently in.

He was clearly delighted with my words, and I remember he confirmed a lot of what I had said as being true. I didn't see David for roughly two years, until he came back for a second reading. He looked so much happier, and was able to tell me that my forecast had happened as I had predicted.

I predicted more for him, including moving away from the area. I saw a blonde girl, small in height with a Yorkshire accent, and although he hadn't yet met her, he would marry her.

Eight or nine months later, I had a dream about David. In the dream he was telling me he had met Michelle from Yorkshire and was marrying her soon. Three days later I received a letter, enclosing a photograph of David and his new bride to be—Michelle, the blonde girl from Yorkshire!

He invited me and my husband down to Yorkshire to his wedding, scheduled for six weeks from then. Unfortunately I couldn't go, due to a prior engagement, but I was delighted to have had a happy ending to one of my readings—and to my dream!

Janice had been having difficulties conceiving a child. She came to me—against her husband's better judgement—for a reading.

I instantly saw what was missing in her life, but was delighted to predict a baby son for her in the near future. She felt this was perhaps too good to be true, but couldn't resist walking away feeling delighted.

Six months later, she fell pregnant—I was told about this by a strange man in a dream. I had met Janice at a social event a few months before, and she told me nothing had happened so far, but she wasn't giving up hope. This man who came to me was able to tell me of that meeting and told me of Janice's pregnancy. Obviously I was delighted for her.

I had a telephone call a couple of days later from Janice to tell me not only was she indeed pregnant, but also that she had just been for a scan and mother and baby .. son! were doing well. I didn't want to spoil her surprise by telling her I already knew.

Richard was one claiming to be sceptical. He came to my office, perhaps a bit unwillingly, with his girlfriend. He nearly died when I began my reading, reeling off events from his past. He has asked me to be fairly reticent about his reading as he's a rather deep person. He doesn't want me to be too candid.

His past was fairly clear, as were the feelings and plans he was having at present. My vibes allowed me to be extremely accurate on these, and he was truly amazed by what I was saying.

Basically he was about to make the biggest decision in his life. My words and predictions fitted his plans in such a way that he couldn't believe what he was hearing. I gave him a two-year forecast and, although everything I said was what he wanted to hear, he left, not feeling sceptical, but excited and more motivated than before.

After his return two years later, I found he had followed my advice and had encountered obstacles of which I had fore-warned him. Because of this, he was able to swerve all obstructions and had never really made any mistakes.

Had it not been for my psychic advice, he would have found life so much more difficult and would not have succeeded with the same speed.

Richard was delighted and was in line for an excellent promotion, very grand for his young years. He is well on track to being a massive success.

Sceptical Richard now comes to me every time he has a dilemma, whether it be personal or professional.

Liz came to me asking for advice on a new career move. As it happened, I did not feel she was making the correct decision and she was quite surprised when I advised her of this.

My vibes were telling me to guide her towards a career involving finance, and she explained that this had been a previous option. However she now felt she wanted something exhilarating.

The path she was considering was coming over clearly in her reading and I was genuinely concerned with all the negative vibes I was feeling. I discussed the path I felt she should go on, and she left my office confused but, I think, still planning to go ahead with her initial plan.

Sadly, Liz returned 18 months later to say that she was struggling with the course required for her new career, which was in the glamour industry. Again, I felt negative vibes (bearing in mind that by this time I had no recollection of her reading a year and a half ago) and I again told her my vibes were guiding her towards finance.

She was clearly an intelligent girl, and the reason for her failure on the current course was lack of enthusiasm rather than an inability to succeed.

She explained that everything I was saying had been said in the first reading, and she now regretted not following my psychic advice.

Now, two years later, Liz has switched course and is aiming towards an extremely successful career in finance. She admits she feels more comfortable with this line of work and is thoroughly enjoying the training and looks forward to her new career.

A local officer, who shall remain anonymous, had been put under a fairly serious charge with his regiment and stood to lose everything he had worked for. He had made a foolish mistake and, although it remained critical, he had an impeccable record and his mistake was a one-off.

Three weeks before his court martial date he came to me for

advice. He was frantic about his future and needed to know the outcome, as he was driving himself insane. He couldn't wait a further three weeks to find out his fate.

It was clear from the vibes I initially got that this wrecked man was petrified about something. He seemed terribly afraid of his future and, as I tried to see what lay ahead for him, I saw only blackness. I had a feeling of dread.

This was due, obviously, to his own current state of mind. As soon as I tuned out of his mind, I began to see the scenario more clearly. (Bear in mind that "tuning" into my client is the first step I must take when I begin a reading. I then reach their wavelength and "tune" out again, by which time I have enough of their own vibes to get me started.)

I could see uniformed men all around him, and everyone had stern expressions. My client looked like the proverbial lamb at the slaughter. I knew then that he was in deep, military trouble.

The next half hour brought out a candid and clear account of what had happened, my client's potential exit from the force and how he was feeling about the entire affair.

Unfortunately I was unable to predict the outcome my client had wanted. I have always been determined up until now, and shall remain so, to give only pure fact from my reading. Many clients don't like what I say, but I cannot simply tell them what they want to hear. That would only prove futile.

I predicted the next four years for my client, and he was initially extremely disturbed, for the reasons I have just mentioned.

What he did admit to me, as we neared the end of his reading, was that he now felt more relieved and, although he didn't want to hear what I had said, he felt he could cope and was more resigned to the outcome.

I predicted that within eight weeks of the reading he would move back to his home town, some 400 miles away, and that he would be unemployed for seven months. Overall the coming twelve months were not to be good for him. He would suffer emotional stress and would have no zest for life. He would lose interest in everything he held dear and, in fact, would all but give up on life.

Beyond that, however, I could predict a new job, roughly doing the same task as he had within the forces, but without the rigid discipline. I also predicted that he would, within one year of beginning the job, be asked to go into partnership with the same firm. He was to prove very successful and before long would be able to put this entire sorry episode behind him.

I think he remained unsure about everything I said beyond the court martial. I don't think he could see any future beyond that point, and he therefore chose to listen to the rest of my reading with half an ear.

However, three years on, my client visited me whilst visiting other friends in my neck of the woods. At first I almost didn't recognise him. He had gained weight—but a nice, healthy amount, not an obese gain. He looked fit and healthy and, thankfully, extremely happy.

He explained that when he left my office three years before, he truly didn't believe he had any future. He was afraid and desperately insecure. He was discharged from his unit and had to begin a new life outside the force.

He left Scotland and returned to his home town where he began a reclusive twelve months, and basically stopped living.

His brother, who had his own small business operating in the same line of work my client did, offered him a temporary job. It wasn't charity. My client's brother genuinely needed the help and because of this, only because of this, my client accepted. He had turned down a few offers prior to this, but his pride wouldn't accept charity. This way, he was doing the favour.

The temporary contract lasted one full year, by which time the two brothers had not only got out of their difficult spell but had also built up an extremely fruitful business. It was at this point that my client was offered the partnership, which he accepted with delight.

He now runs this very successful business with his brother and, in all honesty, admits to being happier than he had been in the forces. He just hadn't realised it.

I always believe everything happens for a reason, good and bad.

Anna loved life. Her entire being was full of laughter, excitement and good fun. I was impressed by her ability to make everyone laugh. No one would ever know if Anna had something worrying her.

The first time she came to see me, her reading was showing lots of change and fairly severe upheaval. Not all of this was bad, however. Some of her changes would prove to be extremely good.

I surprised her by predicting huge redundancies from her well-established firm. Secondly, I saw another relationship, which truly threw her. She had been in a stable marriage for eight years. And, thirdly, I foresaw another pregnancy.

As this was apparently all to happen within two years, Anna

wasn't the only one who felt shocked, and perhaps a little doubtful. I myself couldn't believe so much could happen within such a short time. I even began to doubt the reading myself.

I felt the next two years would be fairly unpleasant for Anna, due mainly to what I've just said, but also because she had so much to endure.

I did, however, predict a far better time within four years, and could clearly see ultimate happiness and a different, better life within that time.

She didn't feel her life was unhappy, and my reading must have caused unwelcome ripples in her calm, serene life. I must admit I felt awful, but had to remind myself that I was only voicing my psychic opinion and telling what I genuinely foresaw.

This was one reading I truly thought I had got wrong. I never did forget Anna's reading, for I was overwhelmed by it.

Anna returned 18 months later, very different from the bubbly, happy, outgoing girl I had met before.

I knew on seeing her that a lot of my predictions had happened. She looked as if she had the entire world resting on her shoulders.

Although I couldn't remember the exact predictions I had made, I could tell that her life had been turned upside down.

The firm she worked for, the well established firm I mentioned earlier, had gone into voluntary liquidation, meaning all employees lost their jobs. Her husband had an affair which Anna couldn't forgive, and they subsequently separated. Her entire life, as she knew it, had gone.

I once again did a reading for her, and this time the predictions were tremendous. I could see a new, more exhilarating career, a new relationship and another pregnancy. The only unfortunate thing was, most of this wasn't to begin for a further six months.

The first prediction to materialise was to be her new career. She would start off in a position of authority, which would be an opportunity she had never been given in her last career. This was obviously to prove hugely exciting. With this new firm she would meet the new partner I had also predicted, and through this she would have the unexpected child.

Again, all of this was to happen within two years. It once again seemed unlikely, but we did remind ourselves of the sheer change from the past two years. If that could happen, then so could this.

It did, and Anna is a more complete and happy person than she was the first time around. Her life has taken on new dimensions, unimaginable prior to her first reading.

A client who was considering opening a shop asked if I could see an ideal location. I had previously carried out a reading in which I advised her to consider a move such as this. I felt that by changing career and following her dream of owning a shop selling ladies' fashion, she would bring herself some long-awaited success and recognition. In answer to her question, I could clearly see a shop selling wall and floor tiles. I knew that this was not the merchandise she would sell, and quickly realised that the tile shop would be leased by her and transformed into her boutique. This proved correct, for within four months of her consultation with me, the lease became available for premises which previously sold tiles. My client felt she may have missed out on this if it had not been for my premonition. She is now in her second year of trade and her business is extremely successful.

Lily and her husband came to me and, although they didn't state exactly why they felt they needed a reading, they obviously had an unanswered question on their mind. I did Lily's reading first and it immediately became clear that she would shortly undergo huge change. I felt a house move would be among one of the many changes. I told Lily this, but wasn't clear on why I could hear foreign languages. It didn't immediately register that they would be moving not only to another house but also to another country.

I didn't feel any, "strange" or "lonely" vibes, which I would have normally expected with such a large move. Instead I felt great warmth and a huge welcome. In Bob's reading I saw which foreign land. They were moving to live nearer their son and his family, in Hong Kong. This would explain why, although this was to be a massive upheaval for a couple of their age, it would also prove to be very happy and would feel more like home than their present home did. They would have their loving family around them.

And, of course, that's exactly what happened. Lily and Bob moved shortly afterwards to Hong Kong, where they are very happy. I think they had this very much on their minds when they visited me. They just wanted confirmation that it would be the right thing to do.

June 14th 1993, saw us all sit around the dining table. I was in a fairly mischievous mood and found myself receiving very strange vibes about Jamie, my girlfriend's latest love.

Jamie was quiet and not exactly the life and soul of any party. However, within the hour, I had him sussed out and knew a great deal about him. It transpired that Jamie was a budding songwriter and deep within this introvert character there lay an extremely talented guy. I was able to see this by vision of his hidden nature, and also by actually seeing his brilliant work. Very few folk knew of Jamie's talent. In fact he went to great pains to avoid revealing it.

I just knew it would be wrong of me, in this instance, to voice my vibes. Instead I waited until we were alone. I know I caught him off guard, and he was dumbfounded when I broached the subject. He did, however, readily admit his passion for writing and although he confessed he felt he wasn't particularly good, he did admit he yearned to write for a living. I pointed out that it was only himself who felt he had no talent, and that if he would let people see his work, then he would quickly see other's appreciation. He couldn't judge his own work without showing it around, I said.

He asked me not to repeat our conversation and I promised not to, so long as he wouldn't ignore or forget what I had said. My vibes promised a way out of his current rut and, by using his talents, he would be guaranteed a far better standard of living.

I received a phone call from Jamie the following day and, although surprised, was none the less delighted to hear from him. He had taken everything I said on board and admitted he had hardly slept thinking about the better life he could have. I know he was apprehensive, but that is only to be expected.

I met Jamie for a proper, in-depth reading, and everything I had felt before came whizzing back. Jamie's future could be brilliant if he would open his eyes and see the opportunities. I knew he was hooked on what I was saying, and most of what I did say made a great deal of sense to him. As he left my office that afternoon, I knew by the spring in his step that he was set to change his life.

Many other predictions were made that have also come to pass. The biggest was Jamie's move overseas. He now lives in Norway, where he does a lot of writing for local bands. He tells me he is very happy with his new life. After meeting him recently I am delighted to see a much more convivial and outgoing Jamie, compared with the quiet and reserved guy I had first met.

This particular story just proves my point about how the paranormal can be used as a guidance and direction through life. It needn't be sinister and frightening, and it is always, but always, best to voice all of my vibes.

Chapter VII
Casebook: Working With Spirits

Mostly I receive messages about the future. But sometimes it is necessary in the course of my work to call and speak to the dead. I have never understood why or indeed how this happens, and I am strongly against trying to find out.

Many scientists and others claiming the same gift have tried to explain it to me. Sometimes they stress the need for me to study the theories of spiritualism and thereby help myself to develop this gift. I always resist.

I believe I have been given this ability from some unknown source, and I should leave it at that. The paranormal should remain a mystery. If all the answers were discovered, then the paranormal would be no more—the very word suggests the unexplained. So I use the gift I have and don't try to look for the whys and wherefores.

One daunting aspect of my work arises when my vibes inform me of someone's past, or focus on a past family member. My client may not immediately remember or recognise what I am talking about, and it makes me look as if I'm wrong —an impression psychics do not like! I have usually found, however, that after some more talk, all is revealed.

Let me give you an example. I once told a friend, without an actual reading, that I could see his father (who had died some four years before) and that the man was telling me of an incident where his son, my friend, had knocked over a valuable clock. There had been a terrible row and the boy had been severely punished for his actions. The father had never forgotten the event, and had been deeply saddened by his words.

My friend couldn't recall the incident at all. Afterwards, he spoke to his mother and learned that I had been told of an event which took place almost 25 years previously. My friend had wanted some sweets which were sitting up on top of the fireplace, beside the clock. But after being told he could not have them, he decided to disobey his parents and proceeded to climb up and reach for the sweets. As he leaned over, he lost his balance and knocked the clock to the ground. As the clock landed, breaking into a dozen pieces, he ran away.

As a six year old child he was terrified and, knowing he had caused the chaos, decided to lie ... as we all did at that age, for fear of the repercussions. Not believing one word, his parents chastised him not only for breaking the valuable clock but also for lying. In retrospect, and totally typical of parents, they felt they had over-reacted. As with typical children, my friend had forgotten about the row within days.

Here are some more stories from my psychic casebook.

Emily made an appointment to see me in my early days as a Psychic Consultant. She walked in and straight away I felt and saw a very sad, tragic aura around her. She told me of a recent tragedy which had left her widowed. Her face was etched with sadness and her eyes brimmed with never-ending tears. My heart went out to her.

It transpired that she had also lost the only child she and her husband had. Their son had died at only four years of age and, by all accounts, his death was very painful. She had never come to terms with her son's death and we agreed that his death was partly the cause of her husband's untimely death.

Emily seemed so lost. She was clearly in so much mental pain that it was beginning to affect her physical state. She was a broken woman. She quickly told me that she wanted to know about her husband and her son. She did not need to hear about the future. That, she said, did not matter.

I proceeded with the reading and immediately felt the presence of a male spirit. When I first saw him, his face, too, was etched with pain. He then cheered up and began to talk of the life he had shared with Emily and Jamie.

I told Emily that the male sitting beside her was undoubtedly the spirit of her husband. As he had mentioned names, she listened with intent. He asked me to mention the rose bracelet, and she started to cry as she registered what he was referring to. The bracelet had been an anniversary gift, given only the day before he died. Emily had not worn the bracelet since her husband had died. The psychical pain it brought was too unbearable.

Mike then continued to talk of many happy days, paying particular attention to the special days. The tears were streaming down Emily's face by now.

I noted after some time that Emily began to look anxious. I realised immediately that this was because her son had not been mentioned, and I interrupted Mike to ask how Jamie was. Mike told me Jamie was with him and that he was fine. He told me that only yesterday Jamie had been given the final dose of medicine from the nurses, and that he was fully well now. I personally found this interesting, for I had no idea that the dead still received medication in Heaven.

Jamie, he continued, had loads of toys and at last he had his electronic speedo. I wasn't sure what Mike meant, but Emily explained that Jamie had always wanted this electronic car game. He had been too young for it while he was alive, but he constantly asked for it. Emily knew exactly why Mike would mention that, for, since her son had died, she wished, oh, how she wished, she had bought the toy for her son. He had a mountain of toys, but this electronic game was the one he kept talking about.

I asked Mike to let me speak to Jamie, and was told that this was impossible as he was still in hospital. (I hadn't thought Heaven would have a hospital, but apparently it did). He did assure me, and asked me poignantly to ensure Emily knew, her son was going to be fine.

Mike then, in a more jokey tone, asked me to ask Emily why she had let his rose garden fall into such disarray. Emily looked a bit guilty and promised her husband that she would attend to it forthwith.

I think Emily left feeling much better. She certainly looked as if she had hope in her heart. Her eyes appeared have taken on a bit of a glimmer ... so I felt I had done some good.

One year passed and Emily returned. This time she was ready to hear about her future and I was able to give her really good news, as I predicted many lovely things ahead. She has since come back and told me the outcome of my predictions. I'm glad to say she is now, at long last, well on the way to recovery.

She has met a lovely man and, although she is not quite ready for commitment, I'm sure he will hang on and offer her marriage when she is ready. Mike has come over in every reading I do for Emily, and he has given his approval of this new man. I doubt she will ever love anyone in the same way as she loved Mike but, if she can find some happiness without him, that's all that counts.

Another such happy incident happened some time later when I had a very distraught young girl come to me for a reading. She had lost her baby, tragically, to meningitis only four months earlier. When this young girl walked into my office, all I felt was an overwhelming need to cry.

I knew by this time that I often reacted by adopting the exact mood of my client, so this emotion wasn't foreign in any way. I was able to deduce that this girl had borne some great tragedy and, as she sat down and I began my reading, it all came to me in a flood.

To begin, I could hear a baby, just a few wee noises, the kind only babies make. Then this got louder, and I was being told by a voice I had never heard that the baby I was hearing had died and the girl in my office was it's mother. The voice then told me that the baby was a girl and explained the cause of her death. I relayed all of this information to my stunned client and, although she was in obvious distress, she continued to listen with a light in her eye that I hadn't noticed when she first came into the room.

I felt unnerved, only because of the poignancy involved, not by the trauma the girl was experiencing. I could see how much satisfaction she was getting, and I knew this would help her come to terms finally with her baby's death.

We both continued to listen, me to the faceless female voice speaking in my ear, and my client to the words I was repeating. It was near the end when the voice identified herself and told me that she was my client's grandmother. She told me she was taking care of the baby and would reunite mother and baby within two years.

My client had tears in her eyes as she left. I had tears in mine eighteen months later when she brought her two-week-old daughter to see me. I now understood the grandmother's message. The new baby had the same spirit and soul as the departed daughter—a classic case of reincarnation.

Liz-Anne came to me shortly after her husband died. The poor girl was distraught and I believe she was in dire need of some sign that her husband was watching over her.

Stuart, Liz-Anne's husband, had died after suffering a massive heart attack at the very young age of 39. She was devastated and, as she had never been given the chance to say goodbye, she had never come to terms with her loss. As soon as she sat down in front of me, I heard a man's voice. He told me who he was and that he wanted to speak to Liz-Anne. He told me to pass on his love and that he missed her. He repeated his love again and again, but never seemed to give me any real proof of his identity which I could pass on.

Liz-Anne knew how much her husband had loved her and I wanted to pass on something real. He then told me about his proposal to her and, as I passed on his words, I realised how unusual his proposal had been. He had taken her out on a rowing boat and, as the weather was so cold, she had to hold tightly to him for heat. He had done this deliberately, knowing how closely they'd embrace. As they neared the end of their sail he turned to her and popped the question. He was shivering from head to toe and Liz-Anne burst out laughing.

His nose was red from the wind and he looked such a state. She couldn't refuse his proposal and she gleefully accepted.

Liz-Anne cried as I relayed this information on, especially the part about his red nose. She confirmed that it had all happened exactly the way Stuart had described it to me.

Stuart explained how much he missed his wife but assured her they would be together again one day.

Liz-Anne seemed more composed after she left me, and I have seen her once since. I'm glad to say she is slowly coming to terms with Stuart's death.

Isobel had come to me with a heavy burden. It seemed she was being partly blamed for the death of her mother. This accusation was being made by some family members, who felt she had not done her fair share of looking after their mother.

Isobel had a husband with Multiple Sclerosis and four young children, so it was difficult to look after her mother while coping with her own responsibilities. The family didn't see this.

Isobel clearly loved her mother and did what she could. Yet she was being made to feel guilty for everything she had done—or, as the family thought, had not done. This poor woman was about to be widowed and left with four children. She'd just lost her mum and she had no support from her family. I remember feeling immensely sorry for her.

As the reading began, we were interrupted by a message from spirit—from her mum, who told me she was very worried about Isobel. She seemed to lay all her sympathies with her daughter and was outraged by the family. The saddest message she gave us was that Isobel would lose her husband in the immediate future. (As it happens, this sad death occurred only 10 days later but was a blessed relief to Tom, Isobel's husband. The once strong man had been reduced to a near vegetable state as his illness took hold.)

Isobel's mum was so sorry for her daughter, and wanted her to know that she held no regret or anger. Isobel was the one her mum felt had been nicest to her—for the time they spent together was so good. With the others, it was rushed and she felt they treated her like a child.

Her mum told me to tell Isobel that she would get her point across to her other children to make them stop treating Isobel so badly. She told me she would go to Helen, one of Isobel's sisters, in a dream and tell her of her displeasure. Harry, one of the brothers, would have a visitation saying the same. Sandy, the other brother, would also have a sign that she was unhappy with their treatment of their sister. If no one else could make them see sense, then she felt she had to do it.

Isobel's reading was mixed and very poignant in parts, but the messages I was able to give her from her mum gave her some comfort. Within two weeks, I heard the sad news that Tom had died. I had "visit" from her mum who told me Isobel would be alright now, and that the family were once again on speaking terms.

Some six months later, a woman came to me for a reading. After I had finished the reading, she revealed who she was. She was Helen, Isobel's sister, and she told me that she had a dream about her mother and was told to treat Isobel better.

Apparently her two brothers, Harry and Sandy, had a visit from their mother too. After a family discussion, they decided they had indeed been unfair to their sister. They are all happy now and giving support to Isobel in her time of double grief.

Most of my clients depend on my supplying proof to enable them to feel their dearly departed are truly with them.

If a medium can prove herself with such specific confirmation, then the clients have faith and are left feeling much more able to come to terms with their loss. David was the prime example of this.

The story began when David's mother-in-law, Mrs Jackson, came to see me ten months after she lost her daughter in a horrific car crash. Jean, the daughter, had been seven months pregnant when the crash occurred and sadly, after hopeless attempts, the medical team lost the foetus.

Mrs Jackson was devastated by the loss of what would have been her first grandchild. Jean and her husband had waited fifteen years for the pregnancy and had been overjoyed when they discovered they were to be parents.

David, Jean's husband, was inconsolable since he lost his wife and baby.

Jean was talking to me and passing on her love to her mother. The best news came when Jean told us she had her baby daughter with her and the baby looked very like David. She told us how happy she was and how much she loved her daughter. The baby's eyes, she continued, were china blue and her soft downy hair was the colour of her own.

Mrs Jackson was crying softly, but her tears were those of joy.

Jean began to ask after David, and seemed delighted when Mrs Jackson promised to look after him. She explained how much he missed his wife, and Jean momentarily seemed quiet. She picked up again as she told us more about her beloved baby.

She told us that she had lost all her excess weight. Mrs Jackson explained Jean had been trying to overcome her weight problem for ten years. This was delightful news to the grieving mother.

I could then hear the baby's noises and passed this news on to Mrs Jackson. Jean told us the baby had a pink cradle, exactly the same as the one she had when she was a baby.

Mrs Jackson asked me if Jean was safe and if she was coping with the baby. Jean's answer delighted her mother further, for she told me that Granny Audrey was helping her.

Granny Audrey, it turned out, was Mrs Jackson mother. She had died when Jean was newly married. They had all been very close, and Jean had taken her grandmother's death badly. It was lovely to know they were together again.

Granny Audrey had been a nurse, so Mrs Jackson knew Jean was in safe hands. The old lady had been so strong, and had a heart of gold.

I asked Mrs Jackson if it would help David to come and see me. She didn't think David would like it. Apparently he was a bit sceptical. I offered anyway, and told her I'd gladly see him if he changed his mind.

Later on that same day, David phoned me and asked if he could make an appointment. I readily agreed, and we arranged to meet the following week.

David was very nervous when he arrived and I tried to put him at ease. He was a mixture of frightened and wary. However, luck was on my side that afternoon, for Jean came over without too much difficulty.

Jean began her conversation by asking for her "Humbug". This was double Dutch to me but I passed it on anyway. David explained that this was their pet name for each other.

Pet names are usually a very private thing, so my clients are hooked from the time I mention them. They realise that I couldn't have made the names up. This was the case with David, although I could still see his mind working overtime. I knew exactly what he was thinking. Perhaps his mother-in-law had supplied me with this information. And he was quite correct to be wary. My job is a very serious one, and has no room for tomfoolery.

I could see he wanted to believe me, but there was still a huge part of him very doubtful. My heart went out to him, for he had lost such a lot and he needed only some true sign that Jean was around him.

I passed on everything she was saying, but she wasn't giving me enough specifics. Most of her messages were sheer anguish, and I wanted more for David.

Suddenly she asked me to ask David if he still had the chain. She still had her half.

I repeated this and David looked up in amazement. Jean then asked if he was keeping her rose bush tidy, and had he stopped stealing the roses. This was all the proof he needed. The chain Jean spoke of was one she had given David five years before. The chain was a "his and hers" and they had each cherished their own part of it. David still wore his. In fact, he pulled it gently out of his collar where it was hidden.

The message about the roses made him laugh, and he explained that when Jean was alive he would pick the roses from the garden and bring them into the house. Jean didn't like him doing this, for she preferred the flowers to stay in the ground. She claimed they lived longer out there.

Jean then told me to pass on the news about Emily. At first it didn't dawn on me who Emily was, for I hadn't been given the name before. Emily was Jean and David's daughter, but Jean had previously referred to Emily only as "the baby".

David gave a sigh, for he explained that this was the name they had planned if the baby had been a girl.

I'm glad to say David left me that day feeling more at peace with Jean's death. He needed proof that his wife was still watching over him and, thankfully, Jean gave us that proof. I feel immense satisfaction from being able to help the grieving at times like this.

Billy was 72 years old when he came to me for a consultation. I wouldn't say I enjoyed Billy's reading, for I found some of his messages rather disturbing. He had an abundance of spirits around him. At 72, this wasn't surprising. He was bound to have experienced death, and quite a lot of it.

Billy was such a funny man, funny in a very humorous way. He had such a lot of character about him and I wasn't surprised to receive many compliments about him from the other side. It seemed everyone loved Billy.

I felt the spirit of his wife, his mother and father, a long time friend and *his* wife, two school buddies (with whom he had kept up contact) and I think I had every member of his social club who had since gone to the other side!! At first the noise was deafening, a real rammie. Billy was delighted to know they had all come to see him. Most of them gave me their names, which I found helpful and which made the reading easier.

I didn't know where to begin with all of these people. I had never before (and in fact have still haven't) felt so many spirits all at the one time.

One of the first audible messages was an entire verse being

sung in my ear of "Flower of Scotland". This made Billy laugh, as he explained he and the boys sang this song often. The noise died down and one male began to sing "I'll Take You Home Again Kathleen". Billy told me this was his father. Kathleen was his mother, and his father had sung this to her often. A small amount of cooing, together with a light clapping sound, followed this song. Billy again laughed as he told me this would be his mum.

He praised the way I described her appreciation after the song, for apparently she would clasp her hands to her chest in delight and out of love for her husband. This was usually followed by a delicate clap of her hands. Such love I have rarely witnessed.

I found, and I know Billy did too, such delight in the knowledge his parents were not only together in spirit but that they had also been allowed the opportunity to carry on their marriage as they had on earth. They seemed to be very much in love.

Anna spoke next. I was under no illusions as to her relationship with Billy. She spoke of Billy as a teenager and proclaimed her deep love for him. She told me how handsome he was and how they had first met. She gave me my first piece of disturbing news by telling me to tell Billy that they would be together very soon. This meant only one thing to me.

I have heard many psychics say they are not afraid of death and that none of us should be fearful. Being a Roman Catholic myself, I was brought up not to fear death.

None of this has had any effect on me, for I am terrified of death. Maybe my concept will change in the future, but right now I'd rather live, thank you very much. I therefore didn't find her words particularly comforting—so much so that I swithered as to whether or not I should tell Billy. At this point I decided not to. I wasn't prepared to risk frightening him. All I did tell him was that they were all awaiting his arrival, whenever that was to be.

Anna passed on lots more information to Billy through me and, thankfully, he seemed to understand everything I was saying.

Young Billy was the next to speak. Young Billy, as everyone seemed to refer to him, was Anna's and Billy's first born. He had died at the very young age of nine. He was now almost forty years old. I could see a very handsome man, and one who bore a great resemblance to my client. Young Billy told me to reassure his father he was not to blame. I passed this message on, and must have looked blank for Billy explained that his son had died while on a fishing trip with him. Billy had been unable to save his son and had never forgiven himself for this. Young Billy's words of comfort were therefore welcomed by his father, although I could see beneath his eyes and I knew there was no real way of this man allowing himself absolution.

Andrew was next to speak. He told me to say the word "predator" to Billy. I did as I was asked and Billy laughed. We both said in unison, "Andrew". Andrew had been Billy's closest friend and they had known each other since school days. Billy seemed particularly pleased that his friend came over.

A few more friends came through at that point, and for several minutes I relayed messages which took Billy back many years. They spoke of fishing trips, their wives, and some other unmentionable charades, mostly harmless.

This entire reading left me feeling really quite exhausted. Billy was a handful himself, never mind the mêlée of spirits with him. I know that, on this occasion, I made one lonely old man very happy indeed.

Sadly Billy died some months later.

Last May I had an uplifting experience myself.

I had been asked by a friend whom I don't wish to name to see if I could possibly find the spirit of her father.

I hadn't met the man, but was aware that he had died some eight years earlier. His death was apparently fairly gruesome.

Jim, the man in question, had been very active for most of his life, but had suffered a stroke at a very early age.

His illness left him nothing short of a vegetable. He couldn't walk unaided, and he needed help with everyday matters. The most frustrating thing of all was that this normally very chatty, humorous man could no longer speak coherently.

My friend and her family had been left to look after a child locked inside a man's body. They found this heartbreaking.

I wasn't sure if I'd manage to contact Jim, but I vowed I would give it my best shot.

Using his photograph, I was able to relax and concentrate on Jim. I called his name over and over again. I prayed that he could hear me.

Within about twenty minutes I became aware of a presence. I asked if this was Jim and the voice answered a very clear "yes".

I told my spirit exactly why I needed to speak to him. He seemed delighted to talk to me. We spoke a lot about the family and I passed on the messages my friend requested.

Jim told me that he had been present when my friend was asking about him, and was trying to let us know of his presence. He had heard every word.

He further told me that he had been at my friend's wedding, which I hadn't attended, for I'd met her after she married. He told me how lovely she looked, and passed on certain bits of information about events which occurred on the day. Most were trivial but they confirmed to my friend that I was in contact with her father.

He told me of his wife's late attendance—twenty minutes late—and how the hairdresser had taken ill on the wedding day. He also told me that Aunt Mary, again a relative I'd never met, had been unable to attend the wedding, and how my friend had been upset by her absence.

He then took on a more gentle tone as he described how beautiful his daughter looked, and pointed out that she wore her mother's wedding ring. He also spoke of his sadness at being unable to attend his only daughter's wedding.

He spoke at great length about his new-found health. He explained he had taken some time to heal but he was now fully recovered and had all his faculties back.

He confirmed that he was with his family most of the time, and he was sad to see how they were suffering. He knew they couldn't see him, but I was to be sure to tell them he was there.

He asked me to tell his daughter that she was to have no regrets. My friend hadn't been with her father when he died. I was to be sure to tell her that her father understood.

I had a lovely visit from Jim, and was delighted to pass on his good news to the family. They were overjoyed by the facts I gave them, and now believe their dad is with them.

Sandy died in a motor bike accident four months before he was due to marry.

His fiancée, Kay, had come to me feeling quite desperate about many decisions she had to face in her life.

Her main problem was the new relationship she had found, for she explained she didn't feel right about it because of Sandy. She was reluctant to get involved, even though Sandy had been dead for almost four years.

She was also contemplating a move away from the area, but again felt she would somehow be letting Sandy down.

It was clear to me that Kay had literally put her own life on hold while she mourned Sandy's death. She was now allowing her guilt to hold her back further.

I could see many bright and prosperous aspects ahead for Kay, but I also knew she wouldn't make any move easily.

Sandy then came through during the reading. This was one instance that I was truly thankful. I was interested to hear what he had to say regarding Kay's reluctance.

As I thought, Sandy was extremely concerned for Kay and passed on his wishes. He wanted her to make the move away from the area, and insisted it was what he wanted. He explained how powerless he felt as he watched her mourn for the last four years. He spoke also of the new relationship Kay was going into, and told of his approval. He explained he wouldn't be hurt by Kay's decisions. It would actually be a relief. He couldn't do anything now, so if Kay made her life happier, then Sandy could rest in peace.

I'm certain Kay absorbed everything I passed on, and I know that she has since made small steps to move on. I imagine her changes will be slow, but at least she has now taken the first step to a happier future.

Victoria had been married to a doctor for 35 years. He died suddenly, leaving her shattered and unable to face life.

When Victoria came to me for a reading, I was stunned by the transformation in her appearance. The change in two years was so severe I might have been looking at a different person. Of course I was not. Victoria had lost immense weight, and her face spoke of a woman much older than her true years.

I was to do a general reading based on a two-year forecast. I was initially upset to see the way her life had changed, and overwhelmed by the aura of loneliness I felt coming from her. She had given up living and was, by now, merely existing.

I could clearly see how productive and stimulating her life had been before Peter died, and how much she had achieved with her life. Now, however, she saw none of her friends. She hardly went out, and basically her life had stopped.

I had never before felt such dread for anyone's future. I pointed all of this out to Victoria and tried to instil confidence and encouragement, but I knew I was wasting my time. I could see nothing but heartache, loneliness and seclusion ahead for her.

I was genuinely concerned, for Victoria was taking in none of my warnings. She wanted only to be reunited with Peter.

Sadly this was something else I predicted, for I eventually saw nothing at all for Victoria. She died eighteen months later. Natural causes were diagnosed, but the friend who phoned to tell me this tragic news also told me everyone believed Victoria's death was due to nothing more than a broken heart.

I'm often surprised by how easily my vibes can cross. I recently did a reading for a lady, somewhere in her fifties. She had been married to her husband for some 30 years and she explained that they did almost everything together. Their hobbies were joint, their trips and holidays were done together, even their shopping was done together. They were very rarely apart.

Maureen came for her reading alone. Unusual, I know, but her husband was of the old school and chose to disbelieve my profession.

I gave Maureen a full reading and picked up on many aspects of career, health and hobbies. I predicted a second operation on her knee, and went into great detail as to how the problem had arisen. I also saw, very clearly, the medical treatment she had already had. I described the pain, as I myself was feeling it. (This often happens during my readings, for as with my clients emotions, I also feel their pain. It leaves me as soon as the reading is over.)

At this point, Maureen interrupted me to say that every single word I had said was true ... except, none of it was regarding her ... it was everything her husband had experienced!!

I then went onto to describe three spirits who had joined us. The first was Maureen's father. I described, with clarity, his nature, his job, even the scar he had on his lip. I then spoke of her mother. Once again, with precision, I talked of her kindly nature, her nursing career, her love of gardening and many other fine details. Then it was the turn of her brother. Was I right in assuming she was his twin?

Maureen let me finish and then explained how well I had described these family members. She talked of her amazement at my knowledge of them. She then explained that, in actual fact, the only mistake I had made was that these people were her in-laws. I had picked up on her husband's parents and his twin brother.

I wasn't annoyed with myself for getting my wires crossed, for I knew the reason. Because Maureen and her husband were so close and had been together so long, their entire lives had amalgamated. I have heard of this happening to other psychics.

I told Maureen, half-heartedly, that if SHE wanted to know what lay ahead for her, she should bring her husband to me for a reading.

I was quite surprised to see them some weeks later. Her husband had decided to come after all.

Once again, everything I said to Bill was linked to Maureen. I gave in depth accounts of incidents from the past. I spoke in detail of the spirits around us and I was surprised to see how fondly they spoke of Bill. (By this time, we both knew I had made the same mistake.)

I tried to be serious and professional throughout the reading but it was difficult, knowing all the time that the reading I was giving was, in fact, for someone else.

Bill and Maureen left quite happily, both of them amazed by what had happened. There were literally no vibes for themselves. I've since heard that all the predictions I gave all happened, the opposite way around.

Chapter VIII
Casebook: Working With Regression

Another huge aspect of my work, and becoming much more so, is the fascinating world of regression, where I transport clients back to past lives. One question I'm often asked is: do I have many male clients? In most aspects of my work, female clients dominate my diary. But, for regression, the tables are most certainly turned. I see many more men than women.

Again, this particular topic could fill my entire book. I love this subject—I find it so interesting and exhilarating. The very fact that my clients can relate to a lot of what I'm voicing only serves to make the experience more persuasive and exciting.

I myself have been regressed, and have found many, many interesting things that most definitely coincide with this life.

When I do a regression, both my client and I must be in a state of total relaxation. As I tune into them (and that means quite literally getting inside their head) I'm almost totally at one with them. Then I see flashes of past life. A proper voice, more than likely one of my spiritual guides, gives me dates, places and times.

I've never failed to regress someone, and I never need to use hypnotherapy. My psychic ability appears to be enough. I do, however, always find myself particularly exhausted after a regression. I warn my client that, although they won't be hypnotised but will be fully compos mentis, they will nonetheless become very drained. They are able to drive home, but I advise them not to have anything too strenuous to do that day.

My client and I look a sorry state after such a reading. It takes around two to two-and-a-half hours. Both of us look shattered, and often we have puffy and sleepy-looking eyes. What a mess! I find it worthwhile, however, and I'm sure my clients do too.

Sally and her husband came for regression one week apart. I had no knowledge that they were related, and remained ignorant of the fact throughout, being told only at the very end of the second reading. It nevertheless amazed us all that so many coincidences came through during their regression.

Sally was first. At this point I had not met Paul, her husband. I began to transport Sally back to 1953, where she lay on her death bed. Her name was Sadie. She looked to be aged 40. In the background I could hear a baby cry.

The child sounded healthy, which is more than I could say for Sadie. Never, in this particular scene or at any time, did I hear Sadie speak. Instead I listened intently to the doctor and nurse around her bed.

It began to unfold that Sadie had just endured a particularly bad labour, and the doctor did not feel she would survive. She didn't, for she died within minutes. I heard the nurse say how sad this was, as the patient, Sadie, had a ten year old son, named Paul. As I came away from the scene, I noticed Sadie's hand had a huge birthmark on it.

The baby had survived and at the time of the reading would

have been aged around 41. The child had been named Emily by her father and her brother Paul. The father was also named Paul.

As I continued with my reading, I realised how very close Sally was to her husband Paul, and also to his sister Emily. There was apparently some special bond between them all, although they could never explain why. I don't think they even questioned it. It seemed they could read each others thoughts, and were unusually close.

At first Sally sat looking puzzled as I fired dates and names at her. She never gave away any of her thoughts, although I could clearly tell something was clicking, and perhaps even making her feel afraid.

I continued with my regression and found Paul and Emily, her husband and sister in law, had played a part in at least three of her earlier lives, going back as far as 1690.

When I have finished a reading, I always ask the client if anything at all makes sense in relation to their current life. Even I was gobsmacked to hear that Sally's mother-in-law had died in 1953 whilst giving birth to a daughter. The family later named the daughter Emily.

Sally's father-in-law had died only months prior to this reading. His name was Paul ... as was his son, Sally's husband. There were 18 years between Paul and Sally, which tied in completely with my dates. The photographs Sally had seen of her mother-in-law astounded her, as it proved how physically alike they were. The family had commented on many occasions that Sally looked more like her mother-in-law than Paul had.

The next couple of events truly amazed me, for Sally lifted up her left hand and showed me a scar, left after she'd had surgery to remove a prominent birth mark. The second and final thing Sally told me, was, she and Paul have a delightful child ... a daughter named Sadie!!

It was all so clear. Sally had been her husband's mother in her past life and had been reincarnated as his wife. Emily, her sister-in-law, had been her child in a past life, the child she had died giving birth to. And, Paul senior, her deceased father-in-law, had been her husband in that life. No wonder they all felt such an affinity.

Around two years ago. I was asked by a friend of a friend to find out why her son had killed himself. I did not know the victim personally, but was given photographs and other items to help me in my psychometry (the art of feeling psychic vibes from a photograph, piece of jewellery etc).

I got many vibes from these items, and felt two things. First, this young guy had always believed from an early age that he would die young. This feeling had grown into an obsession.

Secondly, he was deeply unhappy and, from as young as he could remember, sensed that he did not fit in to this world. He felt and acted differently from everyone around him.

His parents were able to confirm this, saying how different he was from his siblings. His ideas were, by all accounts, very old fashioned. He seldom made plans, even with infantile things like a childrens' party.

We were all further amazed when I was able to regress him through his photograph—and my findings were astounding. In his previous two lives, he had died at exactly the same age, 21! His penultimate life had seen him die through some disease similar to cholera, and in his last life he died in a drowning accident. I wondered if he had some subconscious memory of this and this caused him to feel, or perhaps even know, he would not live to an old age.

This gave his parents some comfort. Although they missed him, and always would, they seemed to understand now his reasons for taking his own life.

Kathleen's story is equally poignant, for she has lost two children to spirit. Sadly, both had taken their own lives. Her son died at 16 after a drugs overdose, and her daughter died by drowning.

I found this reading particularly emotional. Not that Kathleen was traumatised—she was, in fact, extremely calm about the entire thing. This was surprising, and I found it difficult to understand her explanation.

Kathleen spoke with conviction about her belief that her children would come back to her as grandchildren. She had one remaining daughter, whom she knew would have difficulty conceiving (and this has in fact since occurred).

I am a firm believer in everything, good and bad, happening for a reason. But I admit to being amazed at Kathleen's lack of self-pity throughout her bereavements. I'm afraid I would have felt very differently. Her strength was incredible.

I had the presence of Kathleen's two children, and they both agreed with their mum that they would come back as their sister's children. Neither felt remorse for taking their own lives. It seemed as if they just had to do it.

Most of these amazing facts came over before I had begun to regress Kathleen. I felt a bit out of my depth. I wasn't able to comprehend, as a mother myself, how she could be so calm. And, after regressing her, I'm not sure I understand any better.

Kathleen, in her two previous lives, 1780 to 1835 and 1849 to 1929, had lost two children. Her third child, in both cases a daughter, had almost died at birth, but had been saved both times. The daughter in both lives, as was about to be proved in this life, had two children ... a son and a daughter.

The nature, appearance, likes and dislikes of these two children were identical in each life. It recurred in Kathleen's children, and again in her grandchildren. So Kathleen's future grandchildren, one I predict to be born 1997 and the other 1999, will be uncannily similar to her own children who have taken their own lives, one in 1984 the other in 1986.

I can see the logic in all of this but still feel heart sorry for the trauma Kathleen has endured ... regardless of the fact she is to have the children back as grandchildren.

In each life both children have died of the same cause, though this life is the first where the cause of death was suicide. In both prior lives they were victims of a mass death which looked to me like some sort of plague.

Kathleen is remarkably strong, and her remaining daughter knows everything about the reincarnation. She admits to feeling rather selfish and, although she misses her siblings beyond words, looks immensely forward to being able to have two children of her own. Without the supreme sacrifice of her brother and sister, none of it would be possible.

Jonathan, a photographer by trade, came to be regressed. Specifically, he wanted to know why he suffered such bad headaches. No amount of medicine would ease the pain when it struck at it's worst. Sometimes the pain would be so bad that Jonathan suffered black outs.

No medical reason whatsoever could be diagnosed. The

medical profession had given every possible reason but had failed to come up with a cure.

I took Jonathan back two lives. His last life had been from 1893 to 1940, and before that from 1828 to 1878. In both previous lives he had suffered the same pain, though there was no explanation for it in either life. In his previous lives Jonathan had been extremely arty, just as he is in this life. He had been a painter and, as with his photography in this life, his subjects were always people and mainly portraits.

I could clearly see Jonathan suffering immense pain in both these lives—in fact much worse, for medicine wasn't so readily available. I couldn't, however, fathom why he was suffering. It was obvious that his pain was stemming from one of is past lives, but I hadn't so far found out where, why or when.

Then, within minutes, I found myself travelling even further back in time, and I could hear Jonathan scream. I also heard other voices, sounding similar to a chant.

As I was listening to this, a disturbing scene began to unfold. I could clearly see a man, head on a guillotine block, about to be beheaded. The crowd seemed to be getting some sort of perverse pleasure from the scene they were watching.

As I took a closer look, it became all too clear that the man being punished was my client, Jonathan.

I found myself focusing on some of the crowd and overheard two ladies discussing why Jonathan was in this dreadful situation. Apparently he was being executed for treason. Some of the crowd disbelieved his plea of innocence, while others firmly believed he was telling the truth. No matter what anyone said, however, Jonathan was about to die.

Thankfully my vision faded before I saw the actual execution, but I was clearly told that it did take place.

This, therefore, was the explanation I was looking for. Jonathan's headaches were a direct result of his beheaded death in the eighteenth century. He felt this explained a lot and, although he knows he will never find a medical cure for his ailment, he may be able to alleviate it psychologically. It will certainly make it more bearable, for I'm sure Jonathan thought there was something sinister behind it all.

It's very difficult to know in which life Jonathan will shake off these headaches, and why. But I was "told" that 2080 would see Jonathan reborn, so perhaps it will be in that life.

Edward from Glasgow was one of my first clients. He felt he was living in a time warp, and had felt this way from the age of 20. At the time of the reading Edward was 39.

It was clear to both of us, as we began our journey through time, that Edward had never lived beyond the age of 20 and had, in two lives, died at the young age of 19. This would explain why he felt so strange. He clearly felt he had outlived this life, that he was simply "killing" time.

I found this particularly sad, for he was obviously missing out on a lot of life's pleasure, and had been doing so for almost 20 years. His entire character had changed, almost from the day of his twentieth birthday. He felt no different to anyone else before this age, but has certainly felt out of place and has felt no sense of belonging since then.

Edward has missed out on marriage, children and all the other plans he had made as a younger man. He had once been ambitious and convivial, and had been studying for a degree in engineering. Three months after his twentieth birthday, he dropped out of college and has never returned.

The profound sadness of Edward's story is that he may never

regain a love of life, in this life anyway, for he is compelled to feel this way. He truly feels he shouldn't be on this earth and, professionally, I can see why.

In Edward's case, this life is to serve as a change of course. He will live far beyond 20 in every future life. As for this one, he may pay the penalty for that luxury. I know this is no comfort to him currently, but he feels satisfied in the knowledge that the sacrifices he makes in this life will serve him well for future lives.

Chapter IX
My Ghosts...

I remember lying in bed one morning and, not being a morning person, I wasn't doing much more than thinking about getting up. I've never mastered the art of rising as soon as the alarm goes off. It was a cold, winter morning, so there was little light or noise outside.

As I began to climb out of bed, I heard a strange sound. At first I wasn't sure what I was hearing. Then the sound became very clear indeed—it was my treadmill (which was then, and still is, sitting precariously in my kitchen after yet another fad of keep fit!) There was no one else in the house so it must have been one of the many ghosts who share my house, and a fanatic keep fit spirit at that! I've since heard this a couple of times, as have my daughter and my husband.

Another time, about 10 o'clock in the morning, I saw what looked like a black cloak. The figure turned round, and I clearly saw a man wearing a huge beard looking very sternly at me. I can only describe him as looking like an old Chinese philosopher. He wasn't threatening, but in hindsight he wasn't very warm either. I didn't feel afraid, but did wonder if I had done something wrong!

I have one memory which my husband also shares. It was

his first and, as far as he is concerned, thankfully his last face to face encounter with a spirit. For me, it was one of my nicer experiences.

We were through at my family home, sitting talking late one night about nothing in general when my husband suddenly saw something out of the corner of his eye. He turned and stared and by the time he turned back to us, his face was white.

Through the glass door leading from my mum's lounge to the hall, he had seen a smallish man wearing a cap on his head. The man appeared to walk very slowly past the door, almost as if he wanted to be seen. Mum and I both knew immediately who this man was—it was my dad. (I should point out here that in my opinion my dad doesn't make nearly enough appearances. I wish he would come to us more often.)

As Dad died the year before I met and married my husband, Alan had not met him. He had seen photographs, but you'd need to know my husband to believe that this kind of thing isn't something he accepts easily. I'd go so far as to say he doesn't believe in it—or he'd like to not believe in it. Living with me has changed his mind—very quickly!

My mum no longer lives in that house, but during the 40 years when we did all live there, we had many ghost experiences.

We were great ones, being Scottish, for the Hogmanay parties and each year many, many family members would gather to celebrate the next year. This went on for two and even three generations, so quite a number of those who had been to the parties had since passed away.

For the last eight years or so, after I had moved to Fife, mum claimed to have heard the door knock at 12.10am every single Hogmanay. Even I wasn't convinced! However, I was visiting mum one New Year with my family and, sure enough, ten past midnight arrived and there it was, the knock on the door. Mum then explained that not only does this happen every year—she then opens the door and lets the family spirits in. Then she goes back to the door around 4am and opens it again to let them all out!! The neighbours thought she was bonkers!

The last year mum was living in that house (although at that time, she did not know she would move to Fife—even though I predicted it!) she came through to me for the festive season. Unknown to me, she had asked one of the neighbours if he would oblige her by going into her house at 12.10am and opening the door—he was instructed to stand for several minutes with the door open. He was then to close the door and go back at 4 am and go through the whole procedure again! When mum asked him if had done this for her, he said, very pan faced, that indeed he had done as she had asked but that he had seen no one. Mum couldn't help but laugh.

My daughter, too, has had some weird experiences. One time, when she was much younger, she was out playing and I was hoovering in the lounge—something I no longer get much time to do. I was aware of someone standing behind me in the hall and which leads upstairs to the bedrooms. This may sound crazy but the door was closed and yet I could feel someone walking past. I naturally assumed it was my daughter, and thought no more of it.

After some time passed and she hadn't come back down, I shouted up to her. I got no reply. I went round to the back of the house and she was still there, playing in the garden. I asked her if she had come in and she said she hadn't. Some time later, she herself went up the stairs and came back down saying there was a man in her bedroom. I asked what he looked like and she told me he had vanished in front of her eyes. I don't know who this would be as I didn't get a look at him but, again, we felt no fear. We were simply amazed.

I have to remind myself constantly that it's alright for me to love this kind of thing but that others don't always share my enthusiasm. I often forget that people do get genuinely scared.

One time I was doing a reading for a crowd of people at a client's home and, as I walked in the door, I immediately felt death. I told this to my client immediately and, seeing her fear, had to remind her that this death was in the past. I had to reassure her that it wasn't about to happen. She was relieved about this, as her eighteen month old son was in hospital at that time. The evening continued normally, with my carrying out readings and consultations for the people present.

Some four or five weeks passed, and I had a phone call from the client. She was very distressed. She began the conversation by asking if I remembered much about the evening. Did I remember telling her an old man was with me throughout the whole time I was there? (Incidentally, the readings took place in her son's bedroom—nothing unusual in that.)

As it happened, I did remember. And I remembered asking her to check with the some of her older neighbours to see if they might be able to identify this man. She had done this, and was told that a man in his late eighties had died some ten or eleven years previously in her house. The client herself had merely been amazed by this, not upset or cross.

The problems began when her eighteen month old boy came

home from hospital. He went into a complete tantrum, scream-ing that he would not go into his bedroom. At first his parents thought it was simply because he'd just come out of hospital. Then it got worse—he would scream, quite literally until his face was purple. Four nights this continued until the child claimed, "there was an angry old man coming out of the wall at him."

He was genuinely terrified. She had telephoned me to ask for my advice. It was obvious that this old man had roamed the house in perfect harmony since his death. Then I appeared and, being psychic, I had obviously disturbed or even un-earthed him, so to speak. He was unhappy about this, posi-tively angry.

As this family was so afraid, the only course of action they could take was to have the house exorcised—something I have to say I disagree with. I can't help but feel this is a breach of privacy for the spirit, and I truly believe it is unkind. I've had other mediums deny that—but each to his own beliefs.

One of my very good friends burst into tears one day with my thoughtless behaviour. It was very clear there was a pres-ence in the house. I'd had some strange feelings all morning, and had seen shadows. When she arrived, she too saw and felt this. She was petrified. Our cat too was acting very oddly—constantly looking up at the ceiling as if seeing something which either intrigued or scared her.

I was in a playful mood that day and genuinely didn't realise how afraid my friend was of my work. I'd gone through to the kitchen and saw my friend in the next room looking very apprehensive. For a laugh, silly as it was, I threw a pen which landed with a thud right at her feet.

You've heard the phrase "jumped out of her skin"? That was what she did. She literally jumped high in fear. I guffawed and laughed and then suddenly realised she wasn't making any sound. I came through to the lounge and found her huddled in the chair crying her eyes out. The poor thing had been terrified out of her mind.

Coming here regularly, she has since realised, very slowly, that she should not be afraid of ghosts or spirits. I don't know if she is all that convinced—yet!

Much more recently, she had gone in to make a cup of tea and had been distracted by someone tenderly touching her shoulder. She turned round expecting it to be me and there was no one there. She came through to where I was and told me about this experience. I tried to reassure her once again, and at that point we both heard the kettle click off.

I told her I'd make the tea while she calmed down, and she claimed she had not got round to putting the kettle on! I told her she must be wrong and she was confused with what had happened. But an hour later, the kettle did the same thing—clicked off, boiling hot water inside. This time neither of us had been near the kettle. She still comes to visit, but is always on her guard!

I often have friends come round who swear they see and hear things in my house. One time, not long after I had moved here, friends from Glasgow came for the weekend. By the Saturday night, my friend felt she could not sleep another night in the house.

On the Friday night, after we had all gone to bed, she heard a scratching sound. Then she turned around and saw a female standing, looking like she was filing her nails! She was apparently very attractive and was well dressed. She smiled a huge, warm smile at my friend and then simply walked away.

This experience absolutely terrified my friend, and I don't think she got much sleep that night. I hadn't told her but around four or five weeks prior to that, I had exactly the same experience. I was able to identify the spirit as that of a girlfriend I had lost some three years before. I remember the last time I saw her. We were all going out for dinner and as I arrived to pick her up at her house, she was filing her nails. I've not had any more encounters with my friend, so I can only assume she is away "haunting" her own family now.

I was confused some months ago as to why strange things were happening in my house. The stereo would switch itself on. So would the dish washer. The microwave's light flashed a couple of time—while switched off. I also heard my dictating machine rewind—when it was situated a few feet away from me. It was obvious to me that there was a spirit and, although I couldn't identify who it was, I had the feeling it was a child—a jolly mischievous child!

I thought back to the clients I had seen in my house and none had lost a child like this one. I could not explain what was happening until four days later, when I had a female come in for a reading. I immediately saw and felt she had lost her son tragically, at age four. He fitted the description of my mischievous spirit and my client admitted mischievous was a good word to describe him.

The only thing I was left puzzled by was, why had he been in the house before his mum had been for her reading. I often had client's spirits left behind, but always, always, after the client has left. I asked my client about this and she told me she had been scheduled to come the week before, but after a bout of flu, had to pull out. Apparently a double booking had been made, the first for three woman, the second one for four, a week later. The girls had decided to swap their appointments.

Obviously the wee guy had expected his mum to come the week before. I believe he had come to see her, and perhaps pass messages on to her through me. Rather than leave again, he waited the week until she came and decided to amuse himself with all my gadgets, which no doubt were of great interest to him.

I remember carrying out a reading for an old lady, who was adorable. She was typical of a "wee grannie", with her big bust and her kindly, warm face. I felt such a sense of fondness for this lady—I remember being quite overwhelmed by it. The reading proceeded quite normally. There was very little to tell her—after all, she was almost 85 years old. You didn't need to be psychic to know she didn't have long to go—statistics would prove that.

All she really wanted to know was, would she die alone? I felt such sorrow for her and truly hoped within myself that this wouldn't be the case. She had spent her whole life helping other people, so how sad it would be if no one was there for her when she died.

Around four months after this reading I found myself, for some reason, thinking about this old lady. I was sitting reading and I suddenly felt a presence. I looked up to find an old man standing right in front of me. He told me his name was Alec and that Margaret had died. I instantly knew who

Margaret was. She was the old lady I had felt fondness for, even although I had met her only briefly.

Alec smiled warmly and told me there were six people by her bedside as she died. I was so glad that this dear, sweet, old lady had her dying wish granted. I read her death notice in the paper two days later.

Chapter X
...And Other People's

All sorts of people write to me as a result of my columns in *The Sun* and *News of the World*. Usually they have questions and problems on which they want my psychic advice. But sometimes they simply want to share a story or experience with me.

Some of the most fascinating letters come from people with out of body and near death experiences, and those who have had encounters with ghosts. I've saved their letters over the years. Here are some of the best of them:

My daughter was admitted to hospital after a very serious car crash. She was put on the critical list and, one after another, had a stream of doctors and specialists attending to her.

I was told at work of her accident and rushed to the hospital, praying I wouldn't be too late. I was allowed to see her and was shocked by her appearance. She was covered with a mass of tubes and I could hardly recognise her. I was terrified she would die. I was allowed to see her only for a very short time.

Her coma continued for three days. At no time did she show any sign of recovery. My worst fears were beginning to materialise. On day four I had, once again, been asked to leave her bedside as yet another doctor had something to do to her.

As I walked towards the coffee machine, I felt completely alone and began to feel weak. I sat down in an empty room to gather my thoughts. It was then that I heard my daughter's voice. She sounded frightened and I could hear her repeat the word, "NO".

I was thrown into a panic and ran back to her ward. I was faced with at least a dozen medical staff, looking flustered, and I knew something was terribly wrong. Although I could hear all their voices, I couldn't hear one coherent word. They tried to usher me away from the door, but I would not move.

It was a good hour later when I was told what had happened. My daughter's heart had stopped beating. In effect she had died. They had managed to resuscitate her and, although she was still "critical", the doctor felt he now had a better grasp of her medical problem. The outcome was that my daughter recovered fully although, three years on, she still suffers nightmares and horrific headaches.

The incident on day four of her hospital stay appears to make sense to me now. When I left her bedside, her heart did stop beating and, at exactly the same time, I heard her repeatedly cry, "NO". According to the doctors and nurses, she never did speak. Even if she did, I was a good bit away from her ward at the time, so I wouldn't have heard her.

All my daughter remembers is a floating sensation. Then she saw her (deceased) grandmother with arms outstretched asking her to come with her. She screamed "NO" and then remembers seeing me running through what looked like a hospital ward. Then she remembers feeling safe again.

My daughter now feels that she did experience near death, but describes it as frightening. She remembers feeling that she did not want to go. The hospital have confirmed that all the times have matched.

Mrs K.Stewart
Fife

My near death experience happened almost 20 years ago, but is still as vivid as ever. I had to have a fairly major operation and was really very nervous about it. I can clearly remember being given the anaesthetic and remember that I still felt too much awake to have the operation. The doctors continued regardless.

A short while later I felt my body rise above the bed. I felt like laughing, as I had read an article recently where a patient had the same experience. What I couldn't understand was why I was aware of all this. Surely I should not know what was happening to my body? Something was wrong and I felt panicky.

I saw another four doctors come into the room, and one in particular had a very worried look on his face. I could see my own blood all over the place. I felt terrified by now and began shouting down to them, telling them I was up above them. I saw darkness and felt as if I had fallen into a black hole.

The next thing I remember was a doctor's voice telling me to wake up. Again I was engulfed with fear. I didn't feel I could wake up, and seemed to want to tell him I was dead. I did, however, come to.

I was told later by my doctor that they had almost lost me during my operation. My pulse went up to an unheard of rate, and my blood pressure had plummeted dangerously low. The whole incident had lasted less than five minutes, but my experience felt so much longer. I believe this experience was a near death, but I did not enjoy it.

Mrs S.Culross
Perthshire

I had just found out my husband had been unfaithful. As this was not the first time, despite his many promises, I realised he would never change. The only option left for my future happiness was to divorce him.

I still loved him so much, and found myself deeply depressed by the whole event. Although I was given all the usual promises of fidelity, and although I so wanted to forgive my husband, I knew I had to stick to my resolve. In 1985, we were divorced.

I missed having my husband around and, on more than one occasion, almost allowed myself to take him back. During most of these very low moments, I felt the presence of my father.

He had died three years before I met my husband, and had therefore never met him. If I am completely honest, I think I imagined my dad's spirit rather than actually having his presence. After all, I was very down and, when dad was alive, he would be the one I'd go to for comfort.

I convinced myself that dad was with me, however. During one particularly bad day, when I was feeling very depressed, I heard dad's voice. He had a very calming, soothing voice and this is exactly the way I heard it.

At no point did I see him, but I clearly heard him say my name and give me words of comfort. I could smell his favourite aftershave and hear his voice. I sat perfectly still and listened.

He told me I HAD done the right thing by divorcing my husband, as he would have been unfaithful to me again if we had stayed together. He called me by a pet name. Very few people knew of his pet name for me, and he even used the particular tone of voice I remembered. I have no doubt in my mind that this was my dad.

I tried to speak to him, but found myself dumb struck. Everything around me appeared to have taken on a black aura and was completely blocked out. All I felt was dad's presence.

It was a very moving moment in my life, and one which I shall never forget. I will not allow anyone to tell me this was anything other than my dad trying to comfort me.

He has changed my life, as I am now sure I did the right thing. I have more belief in myself, as well as much more belief in the future.

Another surprising thing is that one week later, to the day, I met a man with the same name as my dad. I knew instantly that we had something special between us and I knew dad would have approved. We are now engaged to be married and I trust him one hundred percent. I only wish I had made my move away from my husband sooner.

Pat Cairns
Perthshire

My husband was tragically killed when we were expecting our first baby. I, as you can imagine, was devastated by this and felt that I didn't want to live any longer. I had four months to go before my baby was due, and I lost all notion of being a mother.

My family all did their best, but I just didn't want to be helped. I even considered giving my baby up for adoption. People

111

tried to tell me that at least I would have a part of my husband in my child, but I didn't want just a part. I only wanted him back with me. I felt hatred for the baby inside me.

Each day was traumatic, and I felt I would never get over my husband's death. I stopped eating and was generally very neglectful of my unborn child.

I knew I was causing not just my family but my doctor a great deal of worry. I was so wrapped up in my grief that I just didn't care.

Two weeks before my baby was born, I was given a very strong warning from my doctor. Either I started eating, or both I and my baby would be in danger. I remember leaving the surgery and thinking that I didn't care if I harmed myself or my baby.

I lay in the bed that same night thinking about everything my doctor had said. Still, even though I knew he was right and I was wrong, I felt no inclination to heed his advice.

It was then that I heard my husband say my name. Although I couldn't see him, I could feel his presence and hear his voice. I could smell him and felt I could touch him. He was crying and this made me feel frightened, not for myself, but for him. I didn't want him to be unhappy.

He spoke to me in a very quiet voice and begged me to pick up my life and to please take care of our unborn baby. He told me I was carrying a son and that the baby would look like him. He would have my eyes but would have my husband's colouring and build.

He told me that my baby was dying and that I must take care. He said I would feel much less sad about losing him as soon as the baby was born. All I had to do was take the doctor's advice. He kissed me on the cheek, which I felt, and as I put my hand up to my cheek, I'm sure my hand brushed against his hair. It was so real.

My husband then told me he had to go but he would ensure I was looked after and, although he could never come back, he would watch over me till I could be with him. My baby son was born twelve days later. I love him dearly. He is so like my husband.

Elizabeth Watson
Aberdeenshire

My sister very sadly lost her four month old baby. His life had been short, but there had been no sign of ill health. His death had therefore come as a terrible shock to everyone.

My sister and I are twins and have, on many occasions in the past, experienced similar pains and similar thoughts. We would often think about each other and then try to phone one another. Nine out of ten times the line would be engaged as our calls registered at exactly the same time.

The night before my nephew died I recall feeling very depressed, without any apparent reason. I had this terrible feeling of dread.

I phoned my sister to ensure all was well with her and, hearing she was, continued as before. Within an hour, however, the unexplained feelings came back. I was unable to sleep and felt a terrible mental pain. I couldn't understand it at all. I just remember being terribly afraid of something, although I did not know what.

Around five o'clock the next morning, I suddenly had a premonition about my nephew. He was in terrible pain and was crying loudly. He was writhing about and no one could hear him. I was panic stricken.

To phone anyone at this ridiculous hour would be bad enough, but to phone and say what I had seen would be worse. I could be accused of scaremongering and would, at the very least, cause my sister to be thrown into panic.

An hour later, the feelings became so strong that I felt forced to phone. The phone hardly let out a ring when a strange voice answered. Immediately I knew something dreadful had happened.

I was told by my sister's neighbour that my nephew had been rushed to hospital two hours ago and she was awaiting news. The outcome was that my nephew was pronounced dead at 4.45am.

The cause was unknown. The only symptom so far had been that he appeared to be in a great deal of pain. My sister and her husband had been wakened by the baby's cry.

Anon
Aberdeenshire

My one and only experience with the "other side" happened some years ago. It was really a very funny occurrence. By that I mean funny in both senses of the word... Yes, it was funny peculiar, but it was also extremely funny in the humorous sense.

I had gone to view a house my husband and I were thinking of buying. He was late for our appointment so, using the set of keys the estate agent had given me, I let myself in.

I had an immediate affinity with the house before I had even viewed beyond the lounge. I just felt it was THE one. I walked into what looked like an old version of our modern utility room and found a man cleaning his shoes. To me the shoes were as shiny as glass. Not to him, apparently, because he continued to rub furiously, using a lot of strength.

I was surprised to see him there, and the fact that he was cleaning shoes didn't really register. I asked his name and, in an abrupt manner, he asked why I was there.

I introduced myself and, before I could ask him anything else, he asked me if I was thinking of buying the house. "Well, yes," I replied, somewhat taken aback. Why else would I be in the property?

He continued, telling me the age of the house and how happy a place it was. He described local amenities and how accessible they were and made some very good selling points. He droned on and on, and it was some time before I realised that I hadn't spoken at all.

I continued to be overwhelmed by the house, not to mention this fascinating man. We then heard the bell ringing, and I started to leave to let my husband in. As I turned the man said, "I'm Stan." I offered my hand but, because he turned quickly around, all I could say was my name.

I whispered how gorgeous the house was to my husband, as we walked toward the room I'd just left. When we got there the man had gone.

I couldn't believe it. I opened the back door and called his name. When I looked at the sink there was no trace of his shoes or the polish he'd been using.

I never did see that man again, but after buying the house I discovered the first occupants were a Mr and Mrs Stan Kay. That was around 1915. Stan Kay died only three weeks after his wife, in 1943!!

People laugh when they mention his name. Apparently he

was a real comic, loved by everyone. He was also a bit of a fanatic, especially, so the story goes, about how shiny his shoes were!!

Catherine Hughes
Glasgow

I had what I can only describe as an "out of body" experience almost three years ago. I was 26 at the time and on this particular night was having difficulty sleeping .

The clocked chimed 3am, and by now I was feeling desperate. I HAD to get some sleep. I had an important job interview in the morning.

I tossed and turned, and then started to feel very light headed. I felt myself rise, and was actually aware of trying to anchor myself down. The ground seemed to be getting further and further away.

I couldn't understand what was happening. I do recall thinking to myself that it felt like I was at the fairground. I looked down and could see myself lying in bed. I looked as if I was fast asleep, but I knew I wasn't.

The entire experience lasted no more than about a minute, but as I started to fall I remember my hand shot out and caused an indentation on the polystyrene tiles on my ceiling.

The next thing I knew it was morning. I quickly recalled the events of the previous evening. I know a lot of people would say I was dreaming, but as I looked up I saw the indentation caused by my fist. The dent is still there today.

Will Lasso
Perthshire

Eight years ago I was given a cancellation hospital appointment for a fairly routine operation. At the time I didn't know why the previous patient's appointment had to be cancelled.

I was admitted 24 hours before my operation. Next day I was taken down to theatre.

As I was being given the anaesthetic, I became aware of a man holding my hand. I recall thinking this was the kindly gesture of a doctor, and remember feeling very secure.

As I fell deeper and deeper into a state of sleep, the man holding my hand began to rise above my bed. He then started speaking to me, and I realised this was not a doctor. The man told me his name and wished me luck with my operation. He told me not to be frightened, assuring me my operation would be successful.

As I came to, I fully expected to see the stranger, assuming he was one of the doctors and that I'd had some kind of dream. No-one around my bed resembled the stranger who had spoken so kindly to me.

I asked one of the nurses if there was a doctor by the name the stranger had given me. She said no. I certainly didn't recognise the name, nor did I recognise the man. I was baffled, but thought no more about it. Perhaps the nurse had just come on duty and was perhaps new to the job. She probably didn't know all of the staff yet.

The following day the nurse came back on duty. She came over to me and asked me to repeat the name I had mentioned the previous day. I did so and she then told me that had been the name of the man scheduled to have the original operation ... the cancellation I had. The patient died only five days before he was scheduled to have his operation.

Mrs S.Freil
Glasgow

I lost my brother very suddenly four years ago. He had no

sign of ill health and I therefore felt completely lost without him.

Neither of us had married, and after we lost our mother we bought a house together. We both had full time jobs, but we spent a lot of time together.

The day after his funeral I was alone in our house when I suddenly felt a presence and realised immediately it was my brother. A table lamp switched itself on and the glasses inside the cabinet began to rattle gently, the way they would if someone were walking past.

I stood up, remarkably unafraid, and spoke his name. I felt his arms go around my shoulder and could feel very faint breathing on my neck. I could feel his head brush my shoulder. I asked if he would speak.

Although he never spoke, he did make it quite clear he was beside me. This presence lasted only five minutes. The following day exactly the same thing happened.

This routine continued for several days, until I had to leave the house for a business trip. I asked a neighbour to switch my lights on for security reasons.

When I returned she told me the table lamp was already on when she came into the house. She clearly remembers switching it off the following morning, but again that evening the lamp was back on. She assumed I had a timer switch, and I couldn't bring myself to explain that my brother was putting the lamp on.

Upon my return I also noticed indentations on the quilt on my bed, as if someone had been lying on it. I didn't feel the need to ask my neighbour if she had lain on it. I knew it had been my brother.

He often makes his presence felt in the house and although I have the house up for sale, I know he will follow me to any home I live in.

**Patricia
Glasgow**

My husband died in 1980. We had been a very happy couple who rarely argued. He was the most sensitive, caring man you could meet. I was devastated by his death.

His illness had lasted almost two years and I had to endure his long bouts of pain and then his eventual immobility. My heart would ache for him during these horrendous days, where he could barely talk for the pain. His weight dropped enormously and his appearance was unrecognisable. He seldom complained but simply resigned himself to the fact he was dying.

The one thing he never lost was his sense of humour. He would force himself to make a humorous gesture, even though it would often physically hurt him. The family adored him and would sit with him at every opportunity. He was never alone.

He often asked to sit by the window where he could see his beloved roses. His eyes would dim if they looked withered, and brighten up if they were in full bloom. I often cut and arranged his flowers by his bed. This would please him immensely.

Two days before he died, his complexion took on a rosy look. We knew he was dying, but his new healthy look denied that death was near. He looked younger and so healthy.

The night he died he looked like a young man. His skin had no wrinkles or blemishes and his hands lost their "liver spots". He was the same man I had married almost 40 years before.

He assured me just hours before he died that he would never be too far from me. He told me he would be able to come back to me. He spoke of seeing a bright light and that he must follow it. He died in my arms shortly after.

I don't remember much about the funeral. It all passed in such a haze. I will never understand how anyone can say the expectancy of a death makes it more bearable. I could not bear my husband's death. I could hardly breathe for the grief and sorrow I was feeling.

Although I had never before experienced a spirit, I never forgot that my husband promised he would try to come back. Six months passed and I was still in despair. I did, however, feel that he would appear to me.

I was right. Almost a year after he died, I awoke with a start. It was very early morning, around 3am. My husband was sitting at the foot of the bed. He looked so healthy.

I was so happy to see him. He was wearing an old jumper, one I had bought for him 20 years before. He told me that he had met my mum and dad and that they sent their love. (They both died years before). He also told me that he had met with his own parents.

He looked so happy and for the first time since he died I found myself laughing. He was standing very close to me but as I reached out to touch him, he backed away. We spoke for a long time after that and then he just disappeared. I never did fall asleep again that night.

The following day my daughter and granddaughter came to visit. My daughter remarked on how happy I looked. I told her what had happened the night before. I knew by the look on her face that she thought it was all in my mind. She was by nature, quite sceptical about most things.

It was then that my three year-old granddaughter came running into the room. She exclaimed that "Papa" had given her the jumper she was carrying. He had told her to give it to mummy. She says he then kissed her and walked out of the room.

My daughter was speechless. I had already laughingly told her what her father had been wearing when I saw him. We had both been in the room that my granddaughter was playing in when her grandfather spoke to her and we can both vouch that the jumper was not there at that time.

My daughter still remains slightly sceptical, although she cannot fathom the reason for the jumper's appearance, or for her young daughter's description of her "Papa". I know full well that my husband was proving a point to our daughter.

Elizabeth Thomson
Glasgow

My husband died three years ago and I have been very lonely since. I have felt his presence on many occasions. I'm usually the only one to see him and at first my family thought it was all in my mind.

Six months ago I had a problem with my kitchen sink. The drain seemed to be blocked and the sink would fill up and cause an awful smell. The food disposal unit is something I've never been fond of. I have never got the hang of it and I'm always doing something wrong.

When he was alive, my husband would repair it for me. As the food disposal unit is located within the sink, I wondered if it were to blame. I phoned a local plumber, who told me he would need to fit a new pipe. As he didn't have the necessary pipe with him, he promised to return within a few days.

Two weeks passed and I still had a broken down food disposal unit. I hadn't heard from the plumber and vowed to phone him the following day.

That evening I heard strange noises coming from my kitchen. As I went down to investigate, I found no one in the kitchen. The only unusual sight was my cupboard door, which had been left open. I closed the door and went back to bed, thinking no more about it.

The following morning I discovered my food disposal was working again. I wasn't surprised. As I've said, it was always temperamental.

Four days later the plumber came back, pipe in hand, and it was then that I discovered the cause of those strange noises.

The plumber looked under the sink, only to discover a new pipe had already been fitted. He asked who had done the job for me, apologising for the time he had taken in returning. I explained that no-one had fitted any pipe. We were both puzzled.

The plumber told me the pipe was only days old. It had no marking or staining and this confirmed its age. I don't know what the plumber thought of me as I tried to convince him no-one had been in to fix the pipe.

To this day I still can't understand fully what happened. But I think my husband fixed the pipe from wherever he is. That would explain the noises and the cupboard door being left open.

Mrs McDonald
Fife

My daughter, who is only ten years old, has always been very perceptive. In fact I'd go as far as to say that I'm sure she has lived on this earth before. I even know when it was. She speaks of her grandfather with such clarity, yet he died 15 years before she was born.

She looks at photographs of him taken before I was even born, and remembers very vivid details. For instance, a photograph taken of my father during the war shows him wearing his Naval uniform. She told us that inside his jacket was a pocket in which he always kept a red handkerchief.

She speaks of Clive, one of dad's old Naval buddies, who drowned during the war. She tells us of the countries he visited during the war, and describes them so vividly.

Most of what she has said so far has been confirmed by my mother. The red handkerchief, for example, was a gift from MY gran, dad's mum. I hardly remember my gran, as she died when I was a child. But my daughter remembers her with such detail. Clare has described her and, again, my mother confirms her description.

Recently, while on a trip to Southampton, Clare asked to see the swimming pool she and my father had swam in. I had no idea where this was. I'd never been to Southampton.

As we drove to find the place, Clare commented on how everything had changed. My mother, who had come along for sentimental reasons, sat stunned. The details Clare was describing were exactly how mum had recalled the old place.

Then she saw it!! Or at least, where it once was. She was so disappointed to discover the swimming pool was no longer there. All I could see was a housing estate. Nowhere could I see a swimming pool. I naturally assumed Clare had been wrong, but she was adamant.

"Perhaps they have moved the pool," she wailed. "Can't we go and ask someone?" Just as we were preparing to go back to the car, an old gentleman approached. I saw Clare speak to him, and then call him over. He remembered the swimming pool. The housing estate had been built over the top of it almost 30 years before.

These are just a few of the signs I have had that Clare has in fact been reincarnated. I have never asked her how she remembers these things, nor have I pointed out that she is only ten years old. I think I'd be too afraid to hear her reply. Perhaps one day she will solve the mystery herself.

Mrs Petra Fulton
Kent

My experience is one of out of body. The year was 1950 and I was in labour, delivering what turned out to be twins. No one realised during the pregnancy that I was carrying two babies. It came as quite as shock.

The first baby was delivered quite quickly and without too much trouble. The second baby was causing the problem.

I was in a great deal of pain and before long I had ten medics around my bed. They all looked anxious, and I remember feeling very frightened.

I started to rise above the bed very, very slowly. I was aware of my body lying on the bed and I was able to see what the doctors were doing to my body.

I can't explain the overwhelming feeling of pain and fear. I looked around, trying to see my baby, but it had been taken into another room.

It was then that my mother appeared beside me. She looked concerned and she told me that the baby they were trying to deliver was already dead.

She relayed everything that was going on below but she was speaking slightly ahead of their procedures. For example, she told me another doctor was coming into the room having just delivered another baby. This happened less than a minute later.

She told me the doctors didn't realise the baby was dead and would not know until the baby was fully delivered. This all happened just as mum said. The baby was stillborn.

I don't know how long I was out of my body but I recall coming back down as my mum left. I was very weak for a long time and, of course, I was mourning for my dead baby.

The other baby was a girl and I love her dearly. I named her Lauren. Lauren grew up with some very strange ideas. She often shows signs of being very psychic. She claims to remember my out of body experience and word for word can recall the conversation I had with my mother. I can't explain it, but her recollection is exact. Yet she was only minutes old.

As a child, she would talk about her past. She spoke with clarity about my grandfather, who she claims lived in the same house as she did. She described his work on the railway and how his fiancee died four days before they were due to marry. She explained that this was the reason he turned into a very different man.

I remember my grandfather being very stubborn and very bad tempered. My poor grandmother had a very sad life with my grandfather for, although he was never bad to her, he was never caring or gentle with her.

Lauren was able to tell us where my grandfather had hidden letters from his fiancee. I later found them in a small silver box hidden in a much larger box. We lived in my grandfather's old house, and I was able to find them without too much trouble.

Lauren doesn't like to talk about her "past", but if she brings up the topic, we don't ask questions.

As a child, she spoke without inhibition. But now she is an adult, I think she is frightened to discover the reason she can remember events from a past era.

Nothing like this has happened with any other family member. Now Lauren is a mother, we see no sign of any of her children claiming reincarnation. I do believe we are all reincarnated, but when you are faced with proof, the realisation is rather frightening.

Emily Bulger
Glasgow

My mum, who has always been quite psychic, often has strange feelings about things. She has dreams which, shortly afterwards, materialise into reality.

An old uncle, my gran's brother, had kept perfect health. At the ripe old age of 92 he appeared to have more life in him than some men half his age.

Mum dreamt that her uncle was lying in great pain and was unable to get to the phone. He had a contorted look on his face and appeared to be clutching his left arm—all the symptoms of a stroke.

The following day, mum told the family about her dream and, because she had previously had similar dreams, we did not disbelieve her. Instead, we told the warden at the sheltered housing complex where my uncle lived, and he assured us that he would be even more vigilant than normal, if that were possible.

He made more checks on my uncle's home and, on the fourth night after my mum's dream, found him lying on the floor, trying to reach the phone. Apparently he had only just fallen, and the warden was therefore in a position to get immediate help. We believe the fast work of the warden, along with my mother's dream, may have saved my uncle's life. He recovered quite successfully from the stroke and, I am happy to say, is still a very agile and lively man. He is now almost 98 years of age.

Another incident saw my mother dream that I was to have a baby. My husband and I had been trying for a family for almost two years and nothing was happening. I was in the depths of despair and was convinced I'd never be a mother.

Mum dreamt of my baby son's christening, whereby she could see daffodils outside the church. This was May 1991. I discovered I was pregnant three weeks later. My baby son was christened ten months later, in March 1992. The daffodils were in full bloom.

Andrea Mulligan
Perthshire

Chapter XI
Testimonials

I have received thousands of letters from clients over the years. I would like to share some of them with you.

"I saw Kathleen in the midst of some horrific marital problems. I deliberately removed my wedding band to provide Kathleen with no clues on the state of my affairs.

My husband was working abroad and I refused to go with him. We were currently planning a divorce. Neither of us were happy with the situation but, as we are both stubborn, we refused to admit this.

Kathleen spoke of many different subjects, and I thought she was never going to mention my impending divorce. She spoke of trivial things, for example, an explosion she could see.

I was increasingly uncomfortable and Kathleen was obviously aware of this, for she told me to be patient and she would talk of my marriage at the end. The news was so good, she told me. In effect she was playing cat and mouse. She seemed in control, though, so I left it.

Then, at the very end of the reading, she asked why I was not wearing my wedding band. She told ME I had deliberately taken it off and she could clearly see and even feel the love between my husband and myself.

129

'Why, oh why,' she asked, 'are you not together?' I was speechless. Just how on earth did this girl know my life?

She proceeded to tell me how stubborn my husband and I were and, if we were not careful, we would throw away our chance of happiness. She told me I would move to another country to be with my husband and that, after a lot of words were spoken, we would resume normal married life. She thought we would live in Germany.

She also told me some great news. I would have a son within a year. She even told me I would name my son Stephen. (I hadn't mentioned my husband's name ... he was Stephen).

I left Kathleen's office feeling elated but did wonder how it would all come about. That same weekend my question was answered, for, as I drove home and approached my house, I saw Stephen's car. He had come home.

We did talk a lot and, in fact, finally fell asleep around 6am the following morning. I'm glad to report as I write this letter—from Germany—that Stephen and I are happier than ever. In fact, all three of us are happy. Our baby son, Stephen was born three weeks ago."

Linda, Stephen and Stephen
Dundee/Germany

"Kathleen warned me that I would face a huge bill for work carried out on my windows. Although I wasn't intending any changes, Kathleen insisted that this would not be through my own choice. She repeated again and again that under no circumstances should I pay for this, but that I would be billed for the work. I was totally confused by this prediction, but kept it in my mind.

Only three days after my reading, my neighbour, who had

applied for planning permission to build an extension, was informed of an urgent repair. Apparently the surveyor had noticed a crack running from their wall to ours, and an investigation quickly took place.

The repair work, as it was an emergency, was carried out immediately, and the bill was huge. We were billed for half the cost.

Kathleen's words instantly rang in my ears, and I had the foresight to contact a lawyer before I paid a penny. It transpired that I was in no way liable for the cost and wouldn't have to pay any of the bill. If I hadn't been warned of this beforehand, I would have paid up and would never been any wiser. Now, through Kathleen's warnings, I have saved hundreds of pounds.

I had been to many clairvoyants before my consultation with Kathleen and had enjoyed most. I also have to say that I firmly believe in the paranormal, for lots of the predictions made by these people have materialised.

Kathleen foretold that a small, two figure sum of money would be won and that three others would win the same amount at the same time. I immediately recalled my firm's syndicate with a local football team's pools. This win materialised some eight months later and, as per Kathleen's prediction, I and the three others in the syndicate won £25 each.

I was extremely thankful for another warning Kathleen gave me. She predicted complications for my son's health. She could see chest problems, and said my son would be very ill if we didn't seek medical help. She correctly told of the huge number of colds my son had been suffering, and predicted a severe bout would shortly leave him very unwell. She explained that the cold would take an unusual pattern, and it was at this point that we were to seek immediate medical help.

This happened in exactly the way Kathleen said and, as soon as we were able to differentiate between his normal colds and this one, we called in the doctor. We fully expected the doctor to give his normal advice of bed-rest and hot drinks, and were amazed by the doctor's obvious concern. Something was clearly wrong and we were thrown into a panic.

Bronchitis was diagnosed and the doctors were fearful this would lead to pneumonia. Luckily it didn't but, as Kathleen predicted, the doctors told us we were very lucky. Another day may have seen a very different story."

Colin Simpson
Ayrshire

"My visit to Kathleen left me very disturbed. She warned of infidelity within my marriage and, as I had begged for complete honesty in the reading, she told me there would be very little I could do to prevent it.

I was quite surprised by this prediction, for my marriage appeared stable. She explained, however, that I would be sent to a different town by my firm and that this would be the beginning of our marital problems.

After a few days, I didn't give much more thought to Kathleen's words. Three months later, my firm advised me of internal cuts and told me they were planning to send me to their head office, some 300 miles away. At this point Kathleen's words came rushing back to me.

I did feel extremely upset but wasn't in a position to refuse the move. I had already told my husband about Kathleen's prediction, but he merely brushed it off. He couldn't see this infidelity happening, any more than I could.

I made the move to head office and, for the first month or so, came home at weekends. This began to get more difficult, as the firm arranged meetings and appointments during weekends. Before I knew it, four weeks had passed and I still hadn't been home.

My husband was initially very understanding as he was also busy with work. He, too, had undergone fairly large changes, and now worked very different and much longer hours.

We continued to see each other as often as possible but it wasn't an ideal way to conduct a marriage. Looking back, it didn't seem so bad, for we were both terribly busy and didn't have time to miss one another.

This continued for around six months and slowly, although equally unaware of it, we were drifting apart. It seemed we no longer had the same things in common. Almost seven months to the day from my move, my husband confirmed my worst fears. He had met and fallen in love with someone else. His new love had given him all the things I should have but didn't. He thought we should legally separate.

I was devastated but was powerless to do anything about it. We tried talking and both took extended time off work to try to repair the relationship. We had, however, become so detached from one another that this just wasn't happening.

My husband had not agreed to leave his girlfriend, but instead saw less of her to allow our marriage a chance. No matter how sad we both were through this, we quickly realised that the damage had been done and nothing would make the marriage perfect again. We had no option but to admit defeat. My husband went back to his girlfriend, and I went back to head office.

One thing I did realise through all of this is that no matter how strange and unrealistic predictions seem, if made by the right person they will still materialise. I couldn't imagine my marriage ever ending at the point I saw Kathleen. But she was right in everything she said.

I shall visit her again soon, for I now need to know what lies ahead for me. My husband and I are undergoing divorce and although his relationship has ended, we both agree that damage done to our marriage is irreparable."

Mrs Kate Owen
Grangemouth

"I saw Kathleen in early June '91. I was newly divorced and life seemed so empty. I just did not know what was going to happen in my life.

I was told that not only would I have met my second husband before the end of the year, I would be engaged to be married to him. I was also told I had already met this man, but so far had no romantic interest. I did not have a clue who Kathleen was referring to, and was left feeling very confused.

Kathleen also forecast that my sister would have a son within ten months. This came to pass nine months later and was exactly as Kathleen predicted.

She then told me of a new job where I would undergo some amount of training. Kathleen said that I should expect a bit of confusion around this but that I would settle down within six weeks. She joked that I would have painful throats with this job.

She didn't know how near the truth she was, for three weeks later I was offered the post of receptionist and telephonist. Initially I was to stand in for someone who would return four weeks later but, almost one year on, I'm still there and have already completed the necessary training, which will allow me the choice of a permanent post.

The most exciting part of my reading happened the following November. As I left Kathleen's office on the day of my consultation, I felt quite depressed. She had told me of this new man and the happy life we would share. Due to my frame of mind at the time, this seemed ridiculous and only made me more unhappy.

I was invited to a wedding in November and I immediately recognised the groom's best man. I hadn't seen James for ten years, but he hadn't changed at all. He had the same sense of humour and was still the same sincere guy I knew from old.

We talked as much as we could at the wedding, and I knew from the minute he asked to see me again that this was the guy Kathleen had spoken about. I don't know how I knew, but I felt so good with him that I sensed that we would come to mean a lot to each other.

We definitely *did* get along together and after our sixth date James proposed. I didn't hesitate when I gave my answer. So Kathleen was right about this too. I had already met my future husband, although it had been ten years since I'd seen him. And, within the time stated, we had got engaged.

When I think back to how I had so nearly not gone to the wedding I feel frightened. Fate and the paranormal are such amazing things and should, I think, be treated with the utmost respect. I was so unhappy at that time I didn't feel much like socialising. I wonder what my life would be now if I hadn't gone to the wedding. I have a pretty good idea ... lonely and miserable.

James and I plan to marry in the spring of next year, so everything predicted came to pass. Amazing, so accurate."

Pamela Murray
Perthshire.

"I saw Kathleen for a reading while I was very unwell. I couldn't understand why I felt so ill. I had tried many different remedies to no avail. I had given up hope and in fact merely put my tiredness and irritability down to my age. I was, after all, almost 46. The onset of the menopause was the most probable cause of my symptoms.

I couldn't believe Kathleen's words when she told me she was hearing a baby crying. This, she explained, was the sign she had if the client was about to become a mother. I could not and did not believe her. These 'fortune tellers' get more bizarre, I thought as I left her.

I even advised my friend, who had a later appointment, not to waste time and money attending her consultation.

She did not listen to my advice, however, as she was intrigued by the whole paranormal scenario. Kathleen had been spot on with my friend's reading but I'm afraid I failed to see the attraction. I was outraged at anyone telling me I would be having a baby at my age.

Imagine my surprise when, almost two months later and feeling more and more unwell, my doctor gave me the results of the blood test he had taken. I WAS pregnant, almost five months in fact. Kathleen was the first to know.

I apologised for having slated her good name. I wish to remain semi-anonymous for personal reasons."

Anon
Fife.

"At the time of my appointment with Kathleen my life was not too bad. I visited out of curiosity and expected very little. However, many of her predictions have come true.

The first thing she did was describe my nature. She was exact.

She then spoke a lot about my mum and, when I offered her a photograph of mum, she proceeded to describe mum's nature and her current lifestyle. She said she saw a lot of worry around mum's eyes but, by winter, the worry would have vanished. All of this made great sense to me.

Kathleen also forecast a change of neighbours, which was great news to me as we were having many problems with the current ones. She then told of a court battle in which she could see tears. She explained that the death of a baby would be the cause.

I was to expect great news around April 20, and the name Margaret would come to mean something to me, as well as proving a great inspiration.

I was informed of an operation which my father would have. This, she said, was due to pain around his hips or legs.

I visited Kathleen in January and by April my father had undergone a hip replacement. This in itself lessened my mum's worries, as she had been so worried about my father.

My house was on the market, although I hadn't really wanted to move. I just felt I couldn't stay in the neighbourhood much longer. My relationship with my neighbours had caused so much pain in my life that I thought the only way to end the problem was by moving.

But, before long, they too had decided to move and I was able to take my house off the market. We are now living in harmony with our new neighbours.

My fiance proposed on my birthday, April 21 (only one day out from Kathleen's prediction), and my lovely new boss is called Margaret. Already she has me training for her job. I would never have had the confidence without her. She is both a great inspiration, just as Kathleen said, and a very good friend.

The sad court news caused heartache in our family. My sister's baby died while she was in labour and, as she feels this was due to medical negligence, she is planning to sue. I have another appointment to see Kathleen, as does my very sceptical fiance."

Kate Smith
Fife

"Kathleen told me the first time I visited her that I would shortly change the current college course I was on. I was slightly disappointed, although I did have a gut feeling I was heading in the wrong direction.

She told me I would pass my driving test that same winter. A man entering my life would have the initials KG, and he would come to mean an awful lot to me. I was to have a confrontation with a close friend but I was not to hold out the olive branch.

Within three weeks of my reading I decided to begin another college course. This time I was going to study Business Management. I felt this would give me more insight into the real world and would probably allow me to go further in life.

My driving test was cancelled on the due date because of a severe snow fall, but I did sit and subsequently pass my test the following week.

I met my fiance, Ken Gorman, almost one year later. He is

everything to me and I suppose I have neglected my friends due to the amount of time I spend with him.

One friend complained about this and said some hurtful things. We have now parted company. I doubt I shall be able to forgive her for what she has said and, although I miss her, I won't be the one holding out the olive branch.

So, many incidents have transpired in exactly the way Kathleen said. I believe in the paranormal. I have been given personal evidence as to why I do, and shall continue to."

Miss S.Black
Fife

"I saw Kathleen at a time when I was very depressed. She was able to pick up on most of my problems without my saying a single word. I was given such good advice that I have adhered to everything I was told. Not only was I told how to cope with my problems and how to deal with them, I was also reassured about my life after I had sorted everything out.

I found this consultation more beneficial than therapy, simply because it was so personal and not just general advice. The fact that someone else was able to tell me exactly what was going on saved me the trauma of reliving everything. I was able to believe in Kathleen's predictions because she proved herself by knowing so much about my past. If she got my past and present correct, she had to be telling the truth about my future.

Many people scorned me for my actions. They thought I had gone completely bonkers! I gave up my job within a bank, changed house, travelled abroad twice within one year, and basically pleased myself.

My husband, the main cause of my depression, made some

attempts at reconciliation but I was strong in my resolve. I took on a new perspective on life and now, two years later, I have never felt happier.

I have the feeling that if I had gone to therapy, I would still be as depressed as ever. This way, with Kathleen's guidance and the paranormal in general, I feel a different person. My outlook on life has changed and my prospects have doubled and more.

I'm now in a very challenging career and have just become engaged to a wonderful, generous man. I know who I have to thank for it all."

Petra Langley
Yorkshire

"I admit to being your average sceptic. I visited Kathleen Coutts quite by accident!

My wife had an appointment and needed transport to get there. I had no intention of having a reading from Kathleen but, after some persuasion, I relented.

The first words she used amazed me as she told me about the spirit of my father. She was able to talk not only of his nature, but mine too. She continued to describe problems my father and I had before his death.

I had so many guilty feelings regarding my father and had never really accepted his death. I had wanted to say so much, and now it was too late.

Kathleen was able to tell me that my father held no grudge and forgave me for all my wrong doings. I wouldn't have believed her if she hadn't been so clear on the problems. She really knew what she was talking about. My wife knew very little of my silent grief, so I was amazed at Kathleen, a complete stranger, knowing so much.

She went on to predict many events for my future and I, somewhat reluctantly, have to admit most so far have transpired. Many events and goings on around my work came out clearly in my reading.

Kathleen was able to give not only descriptions but also names of my colleagues. I was dumbfounded.

However, once was enough. Although I enjoyed the reading, I have no intention of having another one. My wife has since passed her driving test, (as per Kathleen's predictions), so I shall have no need to drive her anywhere near a psychic. I now feel more afraid of the paranormal. I'm definitely not in the same category as the sceptics."

Peter
Perth

"As my husband said (above letter), Kathleen amazed us with her psychic ability.

I have always believed in the paranormal and have often had consultations with psychics. Most know what they are talking about and I'm usually given good advice as well as being given future predictions.

The very fact that Kathleen stunned my husband was great for me. I can talk to him much more about any visits I've made to psychics or whatever. He used to scorn, but he now listens intently. I know he'll never attend another consultation, but he does at least listen to what I'm saying.

I think Kathleen has changed our life. We had been so wrapped up in our own lives that we hardly ever consulted each other. The communication between us was nonexistent. Kathleen pointed out a few factors and, more importantly, told us some home truths. We are much happier in our marriage.

As Peter said, I passed my driving test. I'm sure I wouldn't have managed this if I hadn't visited Kathleen. She warned me of the mistakes I was likely to make.

In the main, I was having trouble with the gears. She was also able to tell me what to do, and before very long my instructor passed comment on how quickly I had overcome the problem. I'm sure if it hadn't been for her warnings I would have failed my test ... mainly due to the gears.

I often marvel at those who doubt the paranormal and think how much they are missing. The paranormal offers so much to so many people.

First you have the entertainment side. More importantly, you can gain so much advice from it.

I think everyone, sceptics included, should at least visit a psychic. They need only do it once. I don't think people should scorn their work if they have never tried it."

Kate
Perth

"My visit to Kathleen was truly amazing. I had never visited a clairvoyant before and was quite unsure of what to expect.

I was engaged at the time and had deliberately left off my ring. I wanted to give Kathleen no clues. She spoke a lot about my forthcoming wedding and described my wedding dress almost exactly, commenting on even the minor details. I was stunned.

She forewarned of problems within our first year of marriage and although this was to be expected in most marriages, I was to ensure we did not contemplate separation. She seemed to feel we were in danger of ending our marriage before it had even begun. She seemed unsure as to the problems themselves but was quite definite that they would be bad enough for us to consider separation.

She was right. Six months after we were married, I completely jumped to the wrong conclusion and thought my husband was having an affair. He was seeing a lot of a new girl at work but it was only due to work matters. I disbelieved him initially, and the rows were fierce. It was like a turntable. One minute I'd be angry with Gary and then the next, Gary would be angry with me. He hated me to doubt him.

So many cruel and harsh words were used that it seemed impossible to glue the marriage back together. We then considered separation. Weeks later I remembered Kathleen's words.

I know now if we had separated, we would never have reunited. Not only did Kathleen foresee these events, she also saved my marriage. If it hadn't been for her I would have continued to be unreasonable and would have left my husband.

Thankfully I have now seen the error of my ways and my husband and I now look forward to a happy, trusting marriage together."

Amanda Hamilton
Glasgow

"Kathleen predicted many events which, over the course of the time stated, have come to pass. She told of a forthcoming marriage and, at the time of my reading, I knew of no such wedding. However, some weeks later my son surprisingly announced he was to be married.

She also told of a knee problem for a male close to me. She seemed certain that this problem was going on at present. Again, I knew of no such problem. As I was later telling a close male friend about Kathleen's words, he admitted that it was he who was suffering the knee problem. Very few people knew of it as he hadn't wanted a fuss to be made.

A friend of mine who also saw Kathleen was stunned when she told her to watch out for she was in danger of losing a very valuable piece of jewellery. My friend had only one important piece, and it was also of great sentimental value. A few days later, the safety catch broke and the bracelet fell off. As Kathleen had warned her, she was able to prevent it's loss.

I have never been a great believer in the paranormal, but after everything Kathleen told me and my friends, I am now a convert."

Mrs Celia Hynd
Cowdenbeath

"At my consultation, I was warned by Kathleen that a dreadful mess would be made shortly by workmen. Apparently, as a delivery was being made of a large piece of furniture, my woodwork would be badly damaged. Two weeks after my reading, I had a carpet delivered and, as they were laying the carpet, the workman took a huge chunk out of my skirting board with his hammer.

I was also very worried about my son, who had been out of work. Kathleen assured me that he would have a job within three weeks. He did get a job within that time, and now the worries are gone.

Other changes forecast within my own job have also materialised in the exact way she predicted. I have always been interested in the paranormal and Kathleen only confirms my belief."

Mrs Helen Jamieson
Fife.

"You predicted many changes for my husband. The first thing you said was that he would change job, as he seemed discontented within his present one. You also said he would be working at a distance. One week later he was offered a job in a town 40 miles from our home. He accepted.

You also saw an operation for him. Three weeks after our meeting, he was sent a letter, arranging an appointment for a varicose vein op.

I, too, was rather unhappy and needed a job of my own. You said not to worry for I would have a job within weeks. This also happened, and I'm now employed and thrilled that your predictions materialised.

A friend of mine met you at the same time as myself and you correctly told her she had suffered a miscarriage. You then told her that she would fall pregnant before too long and all would be well. She did fall pregnant and felt much more relaxed after hearing your reassuring words."

Mrs J.McKenzie
Glenrothes

"I saw you recently and you quite correctly told me that although I wasn't sceptical, I was rather dubious. You then went on to say that you only had to say one word and that would change my mind. That one word was, 'fishing'.

Only the evening before I had lain awake thinking about our meeting. I thought to myself that if you could pick up on my one love, fishing, then I'd know you were psychic. I only needed to hear you say that one word and, as I repeated it again and again to myself, I was sure you should pick up on it. You told me you were unsure as to why the word 'fishing' was repeatedly entering your head. I then explained why.

You told me I was about to sell my car, but that I may be in danger of selling the wrong one. The one I wanted to sell was the very one you advised me against selling. I took your advice and now know why.

You spoke a lot about a new business venture, which at the time was a bit of a gamble. You told me to persevere and it would work out to my great benefit. I have, and now my business is booming and getting better.

You also told me of infidelity on my part which has not yet materialised but, after meeting another clairvoyant, was told exactly the same thing. I am now under the watchful eye of my wife!!"

Mr W.Cumming
Larbet

"My experiences with clairvoyants have always been amazing. Everything I have been told eventually materialises.

I saw Kathleen for the first time two years ago. She picked up on many personal problems which I wouldn't like to be published, but she did help me to sort out most of them and to see the way out.

I had been less than content with my life and was desperately needing to move on. My life had become stagnant, so much so that I was taking my unhappiness out on my family .. the very ones who loved and supported me. I just felt I needed some life for myself.

Katie picked all of this up very early on in my reading, and she was able to tell me what steps I should take to ensure a brighter and more prosperous future. She managed to show me that the personal problems I'd been having were not related in any way to my husband, but were instead a huge sign of insecurity and a lack of identity within myself.

Katie pointed me in the correct direction, telling me of everything I should expect, warning me of potential pitfalls. Above all she gave me hope. I hadn't had much hope at all in the last few years and my self confidence was away to nothing.

I realised before long that Katie was actually reading my mind, and was confirming my ambitions—the same ambitions I had put in the cupboard years before and hadn't given much thought to since. I knew what I wanted, but my downfall was thinking it was impossible.

My self confidence had become so low that I thought I was capable of very little indeed ... if anything. Katie was giving me the only thing I needed to make my life better. I left her office that day feeling bright, breezy and a heck of a lot happier than when I'd gone in.

One pitfall Katie did point out was that my family may not be altogether enthralled by my changes. She equally pointed out that, as I had been there for them for all these years, I was to either insist they give me their full support or simply go on regardless. The biggest thing I had to avoid was allowing them to make me feel guilty for neglecting them.

I couldn't help but smile as Katie spoke such wise and knowledgeable words. It was as if she knew my family personally. She didn't, of course.

She was quite right. Although my husband hadn't been bad to me, and I certainly didn't resent my children, I needed my own identity. Until I could find out what that was, I would feel restless and unfulfilled.

The family would never really see or understand this. They were used to good old mum always being there. Oh yes, I could do the cooking, the ironing, the laundry. I could even sit alone as they all got on with their lives. Between them, they had hobbies enough for ten people. Some were learning, others were recreational, but they belonged to them. What did I have? I desperately needed something.

Katie felt that most of my problems, although appearing selfish, were anything but. She was able to show me that my needs were perfectly normal and that I was the only one able to satisfy them.

I'm glad I took her advice for I am now, two years later, well on my way to finishing a diploma in business studies and my prospects are unlimited. I have met countless new people, and I feel so much better about myself. I finally seem to have found the long lost confidence. I'm a much happier and more fulfilled person.

The biggest thing Katie taught me, apart from all of the above, was to be myself. In doing this, I have been able to learn from the past and to move on in a productive, positive and far more assertive way."

Clara Jane McFarlane
Eastwood

"I saw Katie Coutts for the first time in May, 1990. I was expecting some old woman with huge hooped earrings and a black scarf. I was both surprised and delighted to find a perfectly normal looking and very young woman meeting me at the door.

She invited me in and led me to her office. Once there, she began to tell me things about myself which astounded me. She spoke at great length of the problems I was having and the dilemmas I knew I would shortly face. She not only helped me sort out my mind, but gave me sound, psychic advice on which road to take. I fully believe if it wasn't for Katie's gift, I would still be in the same mess I was in then.

I had marital problems, among many others. I was fairly convinced of my husband's infidelity, although I had no proof. I still admire Katie for the honesty and the delicacy with which she confirmed my suspicions. In the hour I was with Katie, I made my mind up to confront my husband.

Initially he tried to deny the things I now knew to be true. But within a short time, he admitted everything. He seemed genuinely glad that I now knew, for he had been contemplating leaving me for this other woman. In his admission, he realised that his future lay with me and not with his mistress.

I quickly realised that I was not totally blameless. I had neglected my husband terribly in my bid to find myself. He could not get through to me, and found me dismissive and increasingly selfish. In effect, I was pushing him away. I strongly believe this to be the case, and it took both Katie and my husband's admission to see this.

Now, some years on and after three further consultations with Katie, I have the happiest marriage and the single most delightful daughter I could ever imagine—another of Katie's predictions, I hasten to add. My life has seldom been better.

That day Katie also advised me on which way to go with my career. I had gone into the reading fully expecting to be told my job would be secure. Although I wasn't happy doing that particular line of work, I did expect her to say I'd stay within the firm for a good bit longer.

She didn't. She told me of mass redundancies which were to happen within three months, and that I would be one of those affected. I was to get out of the firm as soon as possible, otherwise I would be caught up in the collapse. This came as quite a shock.

I had been dreadfully unhappy in my work and had thought about changing career completely. What I didn't expect was to be told it was the right thing for me to do.

Katie gave me dates on when best to initiate these moves and more importantly, dates to avoid. All four of these dates proved frighteningly accurate. There is never a more true saying than, 'forewarned is forearmed'.

I dread to think what might have happened if it wasn't for Katie and the world of the paranormal. I believed then, and still do to this day, that she turned my world around and gave me opportunities, or at least a better chance to see these opportunities for myself. My stagnant life was about to become one of total chaos. Katie gave me not only the foresight but the strength to find the safe and best route out. I shall be grateful to her always."

Nina McBain
Dundee

"I came to see Kathleen last May. I had lost my husband four years prior to my consultation, and had never really recovered. My husband had been drowned or, as I was told, 'presumed drowned'. No one had found his body.

For an awfully long time I couldn't face the fact that my husband was dead. Not finding the body served only to keep my dreams alive.

I had a young son and, although I loved him, I couldn't give him the attention that I should have. My mind was too preoccupied with my husband. I hardly ever went out of the house and never, ever accepted social invitations.

Billy, my son, suffered too, for I wouldn't allow him out of my sight for very long. I was terrified of losing him as well.

Bill, my husband, had been missing for almost four years when I agreed to meet Kathleen. I wasn't sure what I was doing but did feel somewhat desperate. Perhaps she could tell me where Bill was.

I think, in retrospect, I needed to be told he was dead. I wouldn't accept it from anyone else. I made my appointment under a different name, which was awful of me when I look back, but I needed to be sure Bill would come to me.

I found Kathleen very relaxed and, without realising it, actually became quite relaxed myself ... foreign behaviour for me in recent years. Kathleen's cards told her there was no partner in my life, and I could see she was confused by the rings on my wedding finger. I gave nothing away.

She then went on to tell me that, as she was trying to find my partner in the cards, she had a spirit come rushing, almost running in, she said, from the spirit world. In fact, there were two. One was named Paul and the other Bill.

Bill asked how Billy Bunter was. Billy Bunter was the pet name only my husband used for our son. (Paul incidentally was the second person who drowned at the same time. He

151

and Bill were out fishing at the time of the boating accident.) Bill then told Kathleen that he hadn't been in spirit terribly long, just over four years. Paul had been keeping him company.

I still felt unsure. Bill must have noticed this, for he continued to speak about very personal things known only to the two of us. He asked Kathleen to ask me how my rose bed was doing. Then he told her all about the rain that came, so heavily, the day we were planting it. She couldn't have known that.

I was interested in what she was saying, but when she repeated, 'Princess Diana,' I burst into floods of tears. This was the very personal pet name Bill had for me. He thought I resembled Princess Di and used to call me that. No one else alive had known that.

Bill became disturbed when I became so emotional. He quite rightly told Kathleen that I had suffered enough. He explained to her that I was having a great deal of difficulty in facing up to his death because they had never found his body. He told her his body was trapped way below the surface, under some kind of ruin. He doubted it would ever be found, at least not in this era.

I asked Kathleen to ask Bill why he had not come back and told me all of this sooner. Why had he left it so long before reassuring me. Bill replied by saying that it was only now that I was ready to believe this. Only now was I ready to pick up the pieces and move on.

He had come to me sooner, just to comfort. But I was so wrapped up in my grief that I was ignoring all the signs. I can now get on with my life in the knowledge that my husband is still with me and our son."

Clare Keel
Fife

"I visited Kathleen for the first time on March 21, 1991. I was quite unsure of what to expect for I had never attended anything along these lines.

She told me I was upset by a recent death. This was true, for my father had passed away recently. I had yet to come to terms with his death.

She then went on to say just how uneventful my life was. I seemed to be lacking identity.

Kathleen predicted a new position would come my way by the end of the year. She also said that I would find a great personal sacrifice involved with this. Nevertheless she advised me to accept.

She described my children exactly, and gave many predictions for their future. Obviously only time will tell here. The other things she told me have all come to pass and, in particular, her prediction regarding my nephew.

She told me that Alan, my nephew, who at that time was 15 months old, would be diagnosed asthmatic. She assured me, however, he would have grown out of his condition by school age. He would not suffer chronically but would require medical attention.

There were some other small predictions. I would change my car, my mother would visit Canada the following January, my husband would change his job but would not like his new post and would subsequently return to his old job, and my beloved dog would receive very expensive veterinary treatment.

A lot of these prediction did not ring quite true. Now, two years later, they have all occurred exactly as Kathleen described.

I am now working for a large finance company, have my own office, but have to travel over 30 miles to my place of work. That was the personal sacrifice.

Alan, my nephew, was diagnosed asthmatic six weeks after my consultation with Kathleen. Two years later, at age three, he is much better and is using his inhaler much less. My sister thanks Kathleen for she gave up smoking after her son's chest became worse. She had tried and failed on several occasions but realised that her smoke was affecting her son's health.

My car was changed due to the amount of mileage I encountered with my new job. My mum did visit Canada and left Scotland on January 24.

Ben, my darling labrador cost me over £150 at the vet but luckily he is now fighting fit.

My husband changed job after new management came into his firm. He returned after three weeks because the new job was worse than the one he had left.

Therefore, everything Kathleen predicted came to pass after some time. I was slightly sceptical but I am now a true believer in the paranormal. I have seen Kathleen twice since 1991."

Mrs Pauline Johnstone
Glasgow.

Epilogue

Let's begin right at the very end of all time. It is my firm belief that the world will come to an eventual end, as I believe it has ended time and again in the distant past before we humans were there to witness it. The cause will be a planetary fault. An asteroid—a lump of space rock similar to a comet—will come crashing down on the earth and will literally devour and kill every living being on this planet. Furthermore, it is my belief that this happened in past times, and led to the extinction of animals like the dinosaurs.

I do not believe that some one person will push "a button" and end the world.

Although not in our time, I also believe there will be another war, similar to but worse than the First and Second World Wars. This time the main perpetrators will be the Americans (I must point out that I adore America and it's people). As for when this will happen, I feel it could be two or three hundred years away.

On a less dramatic note, although equally important, I feel cures for illnesses such as cancer will be found in the next 20 years. Cancer will be forgotten like the plagues of old, killers no longer.

And finally, the future for Katie Coutts? Who knows, for as with all psychics, it is impossible to predict anything for thy-self. In my case, certainly, I find it's rather like the key and the lock scenario, I need the other person to tune into as I cannot tune into myself. I'm very open to offers!!